Investing in Japan

An Introduction to Japanese Real Estate Business and Practices

Takenaka Corporation

ULI

Urban Land Institute

About ULI–the Urban Land Institute

ULI–the Urban Land Institute is a nonprofit education and research institute that is supported by its members. Its mission is to provide responsible leadership in the use of land in order to enhance the total environment.

ULI sponsors education programs and forums to encourage an open international exchange of ideas and sharing of experiences; initiates research that anticipates emerging land use trends and issues and proposes creative solutions based on that research; provides advisory services; and publishes a wide variety of materials to disseminate information on land use and development. Established in 1936, the Institute today has more than 23,000 members and associates from more than 80 countries representing the entire spectrum of the land use and development disciplines.

Richard M. Rosan
President

For more information about ULI and the resources that it offers, visit ULI's Web site at www.uli.org and www.japan.uli.org.

Project Staff

Rachelle L. Levitt
Executive Vice President, Policy and Practice
Publisher

Gayle Berens
Vice President, Real Estate Development Practice

Anne Frej
Office/Industrial Development Consultant
Project Director

Nancy H. Stewart
Director, Book Program

James A. Mulligan
Managing Editor

Sandra F. Chizinsky
Manuscript Editor

Betsy VanBuskirk
Art Director

Byron Holly
Book Design/Layout

Diann Stanley-Austin
Director, Publishing Operations

Recommended bibliographic listing:
Takenaka Corporation. *Investing in Japan: An Introduction to Japanese Real Estate Business and Practices*. Washington, D.C.: ULI–the Urban Land Institute, 2004.

ULI Catalog Number: I13
International Standard Book Number:
0-87420-920-X

Library of Congress Control Number: 2004099414

About Takenaka Corporation

Takenaka Corporation is one of Japan's largest planning, architecture, construction, and development companies, with almost 400 years of experience in the Japanese market.

The Business Development Department at Takenaka provides comprehensive project management services that address the needs of the foreign investor, developer, or retailer preparing to enter the Japanese market. The department is made up of experienced professionals with overseas experience in property development, architecture, and investment.

For more information about this book or Takenaka, please write or call

Mizuhiko Tamura
General Manager, Business Development Department
Takenaka Corporation
1-1-1 Shinsuna, Koto-ku
Tokyo, Japan 136-0075
Phone: 81-3-6810-5682
Fax: 81-3-6660-6168
E-mail: tamura.mizuhiko@takenaka.co.jp

Web site, Business Development Department: www.takenaka.co.jp/takenaka_e/tpms_e/index.html
Web site, Takenaka Corporation: www.takenaka.co.jp/takenaka_e/index.html

Editorial Board

Contributors of Research and Information

Shinya Sato
Babcock & Brown Co., Ltd.
6F Izumikan Kioicho
4-3 Kioicho, Chiyoda-ku
Tokyo, Japan 102-0094

Gordon Hatton
Senior Project Manager
Bovis Lend Lease Japan, Inc.
10F Akasaka Twin Tower Building, Main Tower
2-17-22 Akasaka, Minato-ku
Tokyo, Japan 107-0052

Steve Kishaba Sombrero
Chief Executive Officer
Chaney, Brooks & Company, Inc.
Pacific Guardian Center, Mauka Tower
737 Bishop Street, Suite 2700
Honolulu, Hawaii 96813

Senji Yoshimi
General Manager, Investment Division
Kane Fenner
Research Division
Colliers Halifax
Halifax Building 8F 16-26
Roppongi 3-chome, Minato-ku
Tokyo, Japan 106-0032

Hideshige Haruki *Attorney at Law*
Tomohiro Kitada, *Attorney at Law*
Haruki, Sawai & Inoue
4F, Diamond Plaza Building
25 Ichiban-cho, Chiyoda-ku
Tokyo, Japan 102-0082

Ryosuke Homma
President
Kennedy-Wilson Japan
NTB-M Building 7F
2-2-9 Shinbashi, Minato-ku
Tokyo, Japan 105-0004

Eiji Akashi
Partner, Transaction Advisory Group
KPMG Tax Corporation
Izumi Garden Tower
1-6-1 Roppongi, Minato-ku
Tokyo, Japan 106-6012

Kazuo Kojima
Executive General Manager
Real Estate Finance Headquarters
ORIX Corporation

Sanko Estate Co., Ltd.
Ginza Sanwa Building
4-6-1 Ginza, Chuo-ku
Tokyo, Japan 104-0061
Phone: 81-3-3564-8011

Reviewers

Ronald E. LaVoie
Vice President
Global Commercial Real Estate (Japan), Inc.
Roppongi Hills Mori Tower
6-10-1 Roppongi, Minato-ku
Tokyo, Japan 106-6115

Christopher O'Brien
Managing Director and Co-Head of Asia Investments
Starwood Capital Japan Operations L.L.C.
Yebisu Garden Place Tower
4-20-3 Ebisu, Shibuya-ku
Tokyo, Japan 150-6018

Thomas R. Schalow
Professor
Department of Information and Economics
University of Marketing and Distribution Sciences
3-1 Gakuen-Nishimachi, Nishi-ku
Kobe, Japan 651-2188

Table of Contents

Preface

For international investors, it is absolutely essential to acquire a thorough understanding of the unique aspects of Japan's real estate industry. Although Japan's huge office complexes, ultramodern shopping centers, Western-style deluxe hotels, and plush residential condominiums may give the impression that Japan is just like Western countries, business is still conducted in Japan—particularly in the real estate industry—in ways that remain uniquely Japanese.

The purpose of this book is to provide readers with practical knowledge of critical aspects of the Japanese real estate business, including financing, laws, governmental restrictions, and related issues. The research team for this project, from the Business Development Department of Takenaka Corporation, has worked closely with Professor Kazuo Nishiyama, of the University of Hawaii at Manoa. During the second phase of the project, the team also sought the editorial assistance of Professor Thomas R. Schalow, of the University of Marketing and Sciences in Japan.

The book is based on numerous interviews with real estate advisers, loan officers, real estate lawyers, and government officials, and on reviews of trade and government publications. To gain their perspectives on the feasibility of investments in Japan, the team also interviewed many representatives of international investment companies that have already acquired large-scale Japanese real properties.

Chapter 1 provides an overview of Japan's real estate industry. Chapter 2 describes the unique Japanese methods of finding and negotiating for real properties. Chapter 3 explains the various ways in which market value is determined, including appraisal methods. Chapter 4 describes land use and building regulations, including the Building Standards Law. Chapter 5 explains in detail the laws and practices associated with leasing land and commercial and residential properties. Chapter 6 describes how real property rights are recorded and reviews the steps involved in the title search process. Chapter 7 describes the various types of real estate financing available in Japan for foreign investors. Chapter 8 explains the Japanese taxes applicable to foreign investors. Finally, chapter 9 describes successful commercial investments by foreign companies that are either in place or planned for the future. All currency conversions are to U.S. dollars and are based on rates in July 2004.

It is our sincere hope that this publication will be useful to international investors planning to enter Japan's real estate market.

Takenaka Corporation

Investing in Japan

An Introduction to
Japanese Real Estate
Business and Practices

Chapter 1

Overview of Japan's Real Estate Industry

Japan is a small country with a total land area of 377,815 square kilometers (145,875 square miles), which makes it slightly smaller than the state of California. Although it is only one-twenty-fifth the size of the United States, its population is almost one-half that of the United States—125.6 million.

Japan is made up of five major islands—Hokkaido, Honshu, Shikoku, Kyushu, and Okinawa—and hundreds of smaller islands. Because about 70 percent of Japan's total land area consists of volcanic mountain ranges, more than 70 percent of the population lives either on the narrow coastal plains that lie along the eastern and southern sides of the main island of Honshu, or in the northernmost region of Kyushu, where the weather is mild and the major cities and industrial centers are located. Geographical and cultural factors have influenced the value of usable land in Japan, leading to distinctive attitudes toward landownership and to unique conventions and practices in the selling and leasing of land.

A large percentage of Japan's population and economic activity is concentrated in big cities. Tokyo, for example, with less than 1 percent of Japan's total land area, has a population of 12 million—nearly 10 percent of the nation's entire population. And, as Japan's commercial, industrial, financial, political, educational, and cultural center, Tokyo contributes 17 percent of Japan's gross national product. Other major metropolitan centers—such as Yokohama, Osaka, Nagoya, and Fukuoka—also have large populations and highly dynamic business climates, and contribute significantly to the Japanese economy (see figure 1-1).

FIGURE 1-1 Population Density

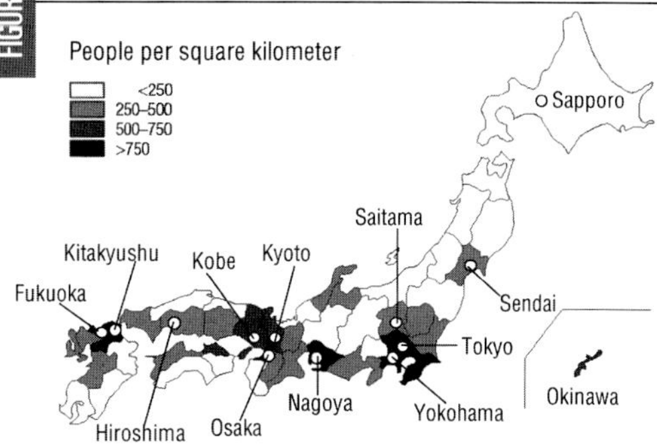

Traditions of Landownership

Despite a sharp decline in land values since the market's peak in the early 1990s, the prices of prime real estate in Japan's metropolitan areas are still very high when compared with those for similar properties in other countries. At the same time, foreign investors are often frustrated by the unwillingness of Japanese landowners to sell land, even at market or above-market prices. This reluctance derives from distinctive cultural attitudes toward land. In traditional Japanese society, the wealth of lords was measured by the weight of the rice harvested annually by tenant farmers, and samurai warriors were given plots of land as rewards for bravery and for their selfless devotion to their lords. Farmers jealousy guarded their ancestral rice fields and other lands, and owners of forests were similarly reluctant to part with their forestlands.

Thus, in the traditional Japanese view, land has an intrinsic value: it is not simply a commodity that can be freely traded for economic gain. Not only does land provide a strong sense of safety and emotional satisfaction, but the sale of land may even be regarded as a shameful and culturally disrespectful act that can harm the landowner's family or corporate image. Even today, the majority of Japan's landowners feel that land is so valuable that it should never be sold, even under

Located in Tokyo's modern Shibuya district, the Meiji Jingu Shrine and its grounds offer 432 hectares (175 acres) of history, tradition, and nature right in the middle of the bustling city.

very difficult financial circumstances. Foreigners considering investing in Japan must take into account the distinctive Japanese attitude toward landownership.

The Real Estate Industry

Japan's real estate industry differs from that of the United States in a variety of ways.

- Significant parcels of prime commercial land in major metropolitan areas are owned by groups of large business enterprises *(keiretsu)*, such as Fuyou, Mitsubishi, Mitsui, and Sumitomo.
- Railway companies, such as Japan Railways, Hankyu, Hanshin, Kintetsu, Nankai, Odakyu, Seibu, Tobu, and Tokyu, own prime commercial lands around their train stations.
- Many large Japanese companies have a real estate division or a separate subsidiary that conducts real estate business for its group of companies and clients. For example, the Mitsui Group has Mitsui Real Estate Sales, a subsidiary of Mitsui Real Estate, which owns and operates trophy properties (such as the Kasumigaseki Building) and many other office buildings in Tokyo and other urban centers. Under the name Mitsui Rehouse, Mitsui Real Estate

also develops and markets residential condominiums and single-family houses all over Japan.

■ Electronics manufacturers, automakers, steel producers, and many other large Japanese enterprises also own extensive real properties. Over the past decade, many of them, especially the ones situated in highly developed urban areas, moved their production facilities to suburban areas in Japan or to countries with much cheaper labor, such as China, Malaysia, Singapore, and Thailand. As a result, foreign investors have opportunities to purchase underutilized former factory sites for their new development projects.

■ Major Japanese general contractors, such as Shimizu, Kajima, Taisei, Obayashi, and Takenaka, not only engage in the construction business but also own and operate office buildings, hotels, golf courses, and resort facilities.

Although some independent real estate companies, such as Mori Building (the owner of Roppongi Hills, Japan's largest private redevelopment project, which opened in Tokyo in 2003), have also been exceptionally successful, the combined effect of these factors is that a small number of large Japanese corporations control more than 80 percent of the real estate industry.

In Japan, the functions and services of general contractors are quite different from those of contractors in the United States. Traditionally, large Japanese general contractors have undertaken all aspects of the construction process, from land acquisition and building permit applications to architectural design and construction. Japanese general contractors have large design departments, and they invest larger amounts of capital in research and development than their U.S. counterparts. As the result of years of cooperation, Japanese general contractors have very close relationships with landowners and subcontractors. Major general contractors are also developers themselves, and invest their own equity in large urban developments. Recently, Japanese general contractors have begun to offer consulting services for foreign investors in the following areas: site selection, land acquisition, project conceptualization, feasibility studies, due diligence, environmental studies, construction and project management, building revitalization, relocation support services, and asset securitization.

The increase in the number of overseas investors in Japan in the late 1990s prompted the development of construction management and project management services. Both domestic and foreign firms now provide these services in the Japanese market.

Governmental Controls and Regulations

Building codes and regulations in Japan are determined largely by its location and topography. Japan is an island chain with active volcanoes and is situated along the earthquake belt of the Pacific Ocean. It is also in the path of typhoons, which occur annually (around October) and can cause heavy damage from strong winds, flash floods, and landslides. About 70 percent of the land is either hilly or mountainous, and the remaining 30 percent—where most of the urban areas are located—is alluvial. Many of the major residential and industrial centers along the Pacific Coast are built on reclaimed land.

Fire is another problem: even in urban centers, there are still many wooden structures situated among tall commercial buildings. The Ministry of Land, Infrastructure, and Transport (MLIT) has put in place strict building codes and other regulations that are designed to protect life, property, and the public health. The Building Standards Law applies to all buildings throughout Japan, although additional standards are determined in accordance with regional conditions.

The real estate industry is also regulated by a number of complex governmental rules and regulations. The MLIT; the Ministry of Economy, Trade, and Industry; the Ministry of Agriculture, Forestry, and Fisheries; the Ministry of Finance; the Ministry of Internal Affairs and Communications; the Ministry of Health, Labor, and Welfare; and various municipal and prefectural governments actively participate in the control of real estate development, financing, sales, and maintenance.

Real Estate Associations

In Japan, real estate associations play many roles: lobbying for the industry, undertaking research, providing consulting services, and holding seminars on industry-related topics. Membership in one or more powerful real estate associations can determine whether a Japanese real estate company succeeds or fails. The associations can be useful for foreign investors as well, providing both information about the industry and opportunities to network.

There is one major national association, and there are several regional associations, all with exclusive membership. The most important national association is the Real Estate Companies Association of Japan (Fudosan Kyokai). Its membership consists of the largest real estate companies, trust banks, and private railway companies, and it has 200 members.

There are two midlevel associations: the All-Japan Residential and Land Association Federation (Zenkoku Jyutaku Takuchi Kyokai Rengo), with 1,000 members; and the Japan Association of Home Suppliers (Nihon Jutaku Kensetsu Sangyo Kyokai), with 550 members. Finally, there are two associations of small and medium-sized companies: the All-Japan Residential Building Brokers Association Federation (Zenkoku Takuchi Tatemono Torihikigyo Kyokai Rengo Kai), with 105,000 members; and the All-Japan Real Estate Association (Zen Nihon Fudosan Kyokai), with 10,000 members.

In addition to these five associations, there are other associations such as the Japan Building Association Federation (Nihon Birudingu Kyokai Rengo); the Japan Real Estate Appraisers Association (Nihon Fudosan Kanteishi Kyokai); the Osaka Land Association (Osaka Tochi Kyokai); the Central Japan Real Estate Association (Chubu Fudosan Kyokai); the Union of Real Estate Fair-Trade Councils (Fudosan Kosei Torihiki Kyogikai Rengoukai); the World Federation of Realtors, Japan Branch (Sekai Fudosan Renmei Nihon Shibu); the High-Rise Residential Condominium Managers Association (Koso Jyutaku Kanrigyo Kyokai); the Japan Wooden House Industry Association (Nihon Mokuzo Jyutaku Sangyo Kyokai); the Real Estate Marketing Modernization Center (Fudosan Ryutsu Kindaika Senta); and the Real Estate Fair-Dealings Promotion Organization (Fudosan Tekisei Torihiki Suishin Kiko).

The Importance of Introductions

When making business contacts in Japan, it is wise to have a proper introduction from a mutual friend or a business associate. Japanese businesspeople are very reluctant to engage in business relationships with total strangers, and it is almost impossible to cultivate a new business relationship in Japan by making a cold call or by sending a letter of self-introduction. Introductions are particularly important in the case of real estate transactions—which, because they are legally and financially complex, involve large sums of money. These transactions usually necessitate working with several different individuals. The person who provides an introduction is known as a *shokaisha* (introducer) and may be a friend of the foreign investor. The *shokaisha* is generally someone who has good personal connections with Japanese businesspeople in real estate brokerage businesses, construction, banking, trade associations, civic organizations, or local politics.

At the ICSC (International Council of Shopping Centers) Convention in Las Vegas, participants discuss commercial opportunities in Japan with representatives from Takenaka Corporation.

Other alternatives are for foreign investors to contact banks in their home country that have a branch office in Japan or a corresponding relationship with a Japanese bank, or to obtain assistance from the office of commercial affairs at their embassy. In some instances, it is a good idea for a new foreign investor to contact foreign real estate companies already doing business in Japan and to ask for cooperation.

Establishing Personal and Corporate Credibility

Foreign investors doing business in Japan must establish both personal and corporate credibility by providing information about themselves and their company. A foreign investor's personal background can be handled in a short résumé highlighting academic degrees and recent professional accomplishments. Corporate credibility is established through a company pamphlet or brochure that indicates the size of the company and describes its main businesses; a brief history of the company and a profit and loss statement should also be included. The information must be translated into Japanese for non-English-speaking Japanese executives.

Foreign businesspeople often ignore the importance of providing enough personal information; what they fail to understand is that before engaging in serious business discussions, their Japanese counterparts need to feel that they know every new business associate personally. It is for this reason that Japanese businesspeople always engage in a rather long social conversation before starting business discussions.

Foreign investors also need to take a team approach. An American investor, accustomed to making deals single-handedly, is likely to try to "go it alone." However, the investor will probably encounter a Japanese team consisting of several members. Ideally, at least the vice president and general manager of the company's international department must accompany the investor on his first visit. The vice president plays a ceremonial role and greets his Japanese counterpart, and the general manager initiates preliminary discussion. The team approach communicates that the foreign investor is seriously interested in doing business in Japan.

Another mistake that some foreign investors make is to send in a young and aggressive manager to make the initial contacts. In the seniority-based Japanese business culture, the manager will be negotiating with Japanese counterparts who are 20 years older or more—and will be at a serious disadvantage as a result.

Due Diligence

In Japan, the due diligence process for real estate investments has not historically been practiced because most real estate transactions were among people who knew each other and therefore conducted business informally. However, the recent arrival of foreign—and particularly American—investors has forced the Japanese real estate industry to adopt the American style of due diligence. (The Japanese phrase for this practice is *duderi,* a shortened version of the English words with a Japanese pronunciation.)

The MLIT, with the cooperation of foreign real estate consulting firms, has begun holding seminars and study sessions for Japanese businesspeople who wish to learn how to engage in real estate transactions with foreign investors. Despite this effort, it would be incorrect to assume that Japanese businesspeople know exactly what the due diligence process requires. In Japan, good real estate properties are not openly marketed, and the necessary information is not readily available. The records of real estate transactions in the registry offices do not include sales prices or the specific terms of sale. In general, the lack of effective nationwide multiple listing services and the absence of escrow companies make it very difficult to collect information in Japan.

A foreign investor who is interested in purchasing a specific building in Japan should first conduct a title search and gather other pertinent information recorded in the registry office. To do so, the investor would hire a "judicial scrivener" (*shihoshoshi*) to go to the registry office, physically inspect the records, and obtain official copies of the documents. The investor must then hire a professional translator to translate the documents into English. Although translation services are quite expensive in Japan, it is absolutely essential to hire a competent professional translator to avoid miscommunication.

The second step is to engage a local engineering company to look into the physical structure and construction of the building to be purchased. The engineers will investigate the building's physical condition, structural resistance to earthquakes, fire-resistant fixtures and building materials, and conformity to building and zoning codes. In Japan, a reputable general contractor can provide this particular service; few independent engineering companies are willing or able to do so.

The third step is to hire a good appraiser who is familiar with the due diligence process. Foreign investors should be aware that some Japanese appraisers still rely mainly on government data for pricing information. Many have adopted the income approach, particularly as project financing becomes more commonplace; however, it is still prudent for investors to carefully analyze the appraiser's report rather than simply accept it as is. (See chapter 3 for more details on appraisal.)

The fourth step is for the investor to inspect the property personally, taking into account the information that has been obtained. If the investor is in doubt about anything, it is vital to ask questions and request clarification.

If the building is a commercial building or rental property, the last and most important step is to carefully interpret the profit and loss statement. A Japanese company and its auditing firm usually maintain very close relations, which has made Japanese auditors reluctant in the past to enforce the strictest of accounting standards. While this practice is changing, very close attention must be paid to this matter.

Foreign investors also need to consider the Soil Contamination Law, which became effective in February 2003—and which, with respect to environmental liability, differs significantly from its American counterpart, the Comprehensive Environmental Response, Compensation, and Liability Act of 1980 (CERCLA—

commonly known as Superfund). In Japan, if contamination on a property exceeds government standards, the new owner is solely responsible for the cleanup costs (except when it is found "reasonable" to hold the past owners or polluters liable). Due diligence is thus extremely important, in order to avoid unknowingly acquiring a property that will require an expensive environmental cleanup. (In the United States, CERCLA holds past and present owners, operators, and managers all liable for cleanup costs.)

Uniquely Japanese Practices

Despite having adopted many methods and procedures from the American real estate industry, Japan has two unique, culturally determined practices that are not found elsewhere. One is the legal protection of "sunshine rights" *(nisshoken)*, which guarantees that residents will continue to receive a specific number of hours of sunshine in their existing house or condominium apartment. To ensure that the necessary legal requirements are met, a developer or contractor must follow specific design guidelines, as stipulated in the law.

The second unique practice is "lease-termination compensation" *(tachinoki ryo)*: if a lessee is asked to vacate leased premises because of impending sale or development, he is entitled to compensation from the lessor for loss of convenience, material and psychological suffering, and financial loss; the amount is between 30 and 70 percent of the total sales price of the property. This practice, established in the wake of World War II as a means of protecting the rights of tenants, is based on the "lessee's right to continue occupancy" *(kyojuken)*. Although this practice is an anachronism in today's developed economy, it continues to be enforced. And, because *kyojuken* applies to all uses of real properties (residential units, office space, or even vacant land), property owners in Japan are very reluctant to lease their properties.

In 1994, Japan's real estate industry, with the strong support of the MLIT, introduced a "specific-period lease system" *(teiki shakuchiken seido)* in order to encourage landowners to lease land for housing development without having to worry about *kyojuken*. One example of this type of lease is the "common fixed-period land lease" *(ippan teiki shakuchiken)*, which is for a term of 50 years or more, with absolutely no lessee's right to extend beyond the specified term. The tenant must remove all improvements to the property and return it in the original condition.

Once home to a large railway freight terminal, Shiodome is now a large city-within-a-city that includes office, residential, and retail facilities. The project began in 2002.

Upon execution of the lease, the lessee customarily pays the lessor a deposit of about 20 percent of the land's value. The lessor keeps this money during the entire term of the lease and refunds it to the lessee, with no accrued interest, when the land is returned. (Chapter 5 includes a more detailed discussion of this topic.)

Support for Foreign Investors

Since the collapse of the "bubble economy," in the early 1990s, major Japanese financial institutions have been saddled with a great many nonperforming loans; this is due, in part, to the sharp drop in real estate values, which returned to the levels of the early 1980s. In response, the Japanese government has instituted a number of aggressive measures to entice foreign direct investment. In 1992, for example, to promote the entry of foreign firms into the Japanese market, Japan enacted the Law on Extraordinary Measures for the Promotion of Imports and Facilitation of Foreign Direct Investment in Japan. Foreign firms that qualify as "specially designated inward investors" are eligible for special tax incentives and loan guarantees. Furthermore, they may also qualify for low-interest loans from the Development Bank of Japan. In January 2003, Japan's prime minister, Junichiro Koizumi, also announced a new government initiative to promote foreign direct investment into Japan, with the aim of doubling total foreign investment in Japan within five years.

At present, benefits available to foreign investors include the privilege of carrying over losses for up to ten years, as long as the losses are experienced within five years of the start of activities in Japan. In addition, for loans received

FIGURE 1-2

Unique Aspects of Japanese Real Estate Practices

Many business practices in the Japanese real estate industry are not found in the United States or other countries. These practices are briefly outlined in the chart that follows and are dealt with in greater detail in the remainder of the book.

Customs, laws, and practices	
Ownership of land	Emphasis on intrinsic rather than on commercial value
Sunshine rights	A certain number of hours of sunshine are guaranteed to residents
Lessees' rights	Lessees have strong rights to continue occupancy; eviction compensation is often required
Real estate system	
Real estate associations	No single nationwide real estate association, but many different associations
Licensed real estate agents	One licensed real estate agent for every five sales staff for companies engaging in real estate transactions; no broker–salesperson distinction
Multiple listings	No comprehensive industrywide system
Escrow system	Nonexistent; tasks are handled by judicial scriveners and attorneys
Title insurance	Nonexistent
Land price determination	Different government agencies provide appraisal information ("posted price," "standard price," and "roadside price")
Negotiations and transactions	
Negotiation process	Conducted verbally, without exchange of written offers
Attorneys	Not usually present at negotiation process
Leasing practices	
Key money	Nonrefundable deposit often paid to landlord
Maintenance fees	Arbitrary and not necessarily based on actual expenses
Taxes	Not passed on to tenants
Office lease terms	Generally not longer than two years
Rental increases	May be imposed in response to unforeseen economic conditions
Assistance for foreign investors	
Foreign direct investments	Foreign investors gain tax incentives and access to Japanese government loans
Development Bank of Japan	Provides financial services and consulting advice

Continued

FIGURE 1-2

Unique Aspects of Japanese Real Estate Practices (continued)

Laws	
Structural safety laws	Strict building regulations to protect against fires and earthquakes
Large-Scale Retail Store Location Law	Special restrictions govern retail stores with sales floors of more than 1,000 square meters (10,765 square feet)
Special-Purpose Company Law	Allows securitization of real property
Real estate investment trusts	Available but still in early stage of development as an investment vehicle
Foreclosure system	Courts take over properties and sell to a third party in order to recover funds
Taxes	
Consumption tax	5 percent tax on buildings
Stamp tax	Based on transaction; maximum is ¥540,000 ($4,800)
Registration and license tax	Based on the assessed value of real property as recorded in the official registry
Real property acquisition tax	3 percent of the purchase price (until 2006)
Special landholding tax	3 percent for land acquisition; 1.4 percent for landholding (temporarily suspended)
Fixed-asset tax	1.4–2.1 percent of assessed value (for properties above a specified size)
Urban planning tax	0.3 percent of assessed value (maximum set by each municipality)

in the first five years after the start of activities in Japan, foreign investors are eligible for loan guarantees from the Japanese Fund for the Improvement of the Industrial Infrastructure. Guarantees may be no more than 95 percent of the amount borrowed, with a maximum of ¥1 billion ($9,235,000), and are available only for loans used to purchase equipment or to finance current operational costs. The guarantee period is ten years in the case of equipment and five years in the case of operational costs.

In the 22 areas known as Foreign Access Zones (FAZs), foreign investors can enjoy loans at reduced interest rates, exemption from local taxes, increased rates of depreciation, and loan guarantees backed by government funds. FAZs are situated mainly around ports or airports.

The following are other programs that support foreign investors:

- International business exchange facilities, such as the Japan Business Center (in Chiba), the Rinku Gate Tower Building (in Osaka), and the Shonan Village Center (in Kanagawa).

■ Japan External Trade Organization (JETRO) Information Service for Inward Investment into Japan, which provides advisory services, information related to inward investment, and symposia for foreign businesses. JETRO also operates Invest Business Support Centers (IBSCs) around Japan, where overseas investors can access a wide range of support services and facilities even if they have never conducted business in Japan and cannot speak Japanese. IBSCs are located in Tokyo, Yokohama, Osaka, Nagoya, Fukuoka, and Kobe.

■ Foreign Investment in Japan Development Corporation (FIND), a quasi-governmental organization, started in 1993, that is staffed by accountants, lawyers, and other professionals who provide market entry and business development services.

Figure 1-3 shows the patterns of direct foreign investment in Japan between 1994 and 2002.

FIGURE 1-3 **Direct Foreign Investment in Japan**

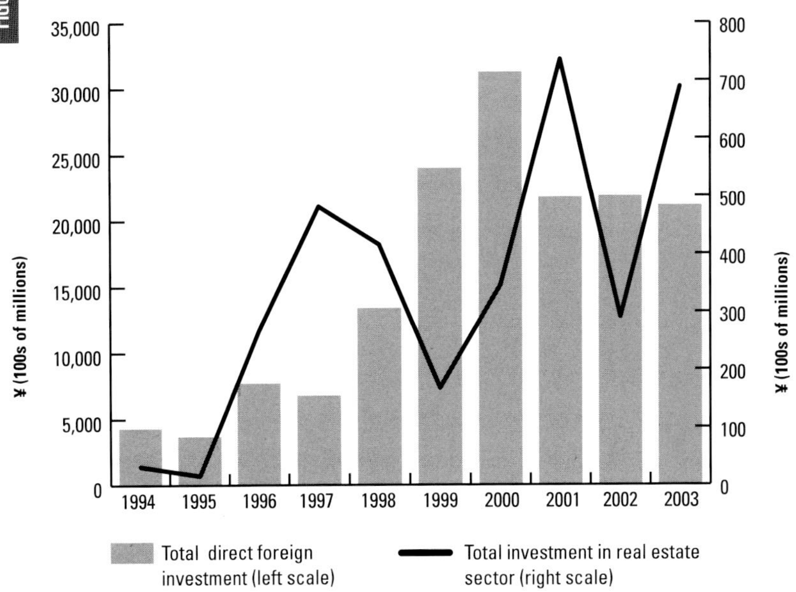

Source: Ministry of Finance, Japan.

Chapter 2

Finding Real Property and Negotiating Its Purchase

Finding a good investment property in Japan and negotiating its acquisition are not easy tasks for foreign investors. The traditional Japanese practice of marketing real estate by word of mouth *(kuchikomi)* is still used extensively, and most Japanese property owners are reluctant to sign written listing contracts and put their properties on the open market. Instead, they prefer to arrange a sale by talking to close friends or business associates. Even under strong pressure from their creditors, Japanese property owners will still resist making information about a property more widely available. Many of the best listings are known as "pocket listings"—properties that are confidentially offered for sale by word of mouth among members of *keiretsu* (groups of large business enterprises) and their close associates.

Despite recent efforts on the part of the Japanese real estate industry and the Japanese Ministry of Land, Infrastructure, and Transport (MLIT) to streamline the marketing system for real properties, it is still very difficult to obtain information on potential investment properties and recent transactions. A multiple listing system, of the sort that exists throughout the United States, has not yet been developed in Japan, and the absence of multiple listings makes it difficult for foreign investors to find good investment properties unless they can establish close business relationships with one of the major Japanese real estate companies.

In theory, the Real Estate Information Network System (Fudosan Ryutsu Hyojun Joho Shisutemu), or REINS, should be the best source for reliable information on real properties for sale or lease; however, this is not always the case. Foreign investors can obtain access to the REINS through a Japanese member real estate company.

Foreign investors should anticipate having to use a variety of informal sources to obtain information on the availability of properties. Large, reputable Japanese real estate companies are among the best sources of information, along with lenders, such as Japanese banks and life insurance companies. Large general contractors, who often have extensive lists of former and current clients, are another valuable source of information. Such firms are also very familiar with the

Foreign investors must adapt to Japanese-style negotiations, which are conducted very differently from those that most foreign investors are used to.

characteristics of their clients' buildings, including the design, architecture, engineering, construction materials, and soil conditions of the site. International real estate companies and foreign banks doing business in Japan are also good sources of information. They all have good working relationships with their Japanese counterparts, and often receive referrals *(hikiai)* from Japanese sources.

Regardless of the information sources foreign investors use, it is essential for them to establish good personal relationships with their Japanese business associates. Foreign investors must also learn how to skillfully take part in Japanese-style negotiations, which are conducted very differently from those that most foreign investors are accustomed to.

Licensing and Functions of Real Estate Brokers

In the United States, any person who engages in providing information, showing properties, negotiating sales, or leasing or managing a real property must be a licensed broker, salesperson, or property manager. In Japan, however, people engaged in real estate transactions are not necessarily licensed.

A realty licensee is called *takuchi tatemono torihiki shunin,* which means "residential land and building transaction manager." Every licensee must successfully complete the designated course of study and pass the licensing examination given by the MLIT. Since there is no broker–salesperson distinction, as there is in the United States, the licensee acts as a broker-in-charge. Non-Japanese individuals are eligible to take the licensing exam; however, they must be residents of Japan and hold an Alien Registration Card.

The licensing of real estate businesses is regulated by the Minister of Land, Infrastructure, and Transport or by the governor of the prefecture. A foreign real estate company must register as a Japanese corporation to qualify for a broker's license. An alternative is to form a joint venture with a Japanese company. For example, in 1999, CB Richard Ellis formed a capital alliance with Ikoma Shoji to form Ikoma CB Richard Ellis.

Current real estate law in Japan requires companies that engage in real estate transactions to have one licensed real estate agent for every five staff members; unlicensed members are allowed to engage in real estate transactions under close supervision of the real estate agent. The main office must post a business-guarantee bond of ¥10 million ($92,350), and each branch must post a business-guarantee bond of ¥5 million ($46,175).

There are approximately 127,000 licensed real estate companies in Japan, with the highest numbers in the Tokyo (25,600) and Osaka (13,200) metropolitan areas, and the Kanagawa (8,600) and Saitama (6,600) prefectures; there are smaller numbers in other prefectures. In addition to the real estate offices found at almost all large Japanese conglomerates, there are many small, independent real estate companies with extensive grapevines for gathering information on real estate deals. These small real estate companies typically engage in small transactions—for example, reselling single-family homes and condominiums or leasing office space and residential units. They may also, under informal arrangements, work as subagents for larger real estate companies or general contractors, buying up small parcels of land.

The smaller real estate companies usually have offices on main streets and have full-page advertisements of real properties for sale or rent pasted on their windows and doors. The real estate agents working for such companies have a broad network of contacts and can be good sources of up-to-date information on real properties within their districts.

Another function that some real estate agents perform is "consolidation of land parcels" *(jiage)*. The companies engaged in these transactions are called *jiageya;* during the bubble economy, they became notorious for using unethical (and often forceful) means to make reluctant landowners sell their property.

Agency Contracts and Conditions

In Japan, real estate investors often begin their purchase negotiations informally, by talking to the seller's representative or to others who claim to have information about a real property to be sold. Japanese property owners typically talk to several friends and business associates, informally and confidentially, about their intent to sell—and, unlike their American counterparts, do not readily sign an exclusive right-to-sell agreement with one real estate brokerage company. The practice of discussing a property sale informally often complicates matters because those who have merely heard about the sale may pretend that they have been asked to help the owner sell the property. Such people are called *anko*—"the sweet filling in the bun"—and need to be taken care of financially if they seem to be helping the owner in some capacity.

In addition, in Japan, buyers and sellers do not exchange written offers and counteroffers. As a result, almost all negotiations are conducted verbally and concluded in the course of many negotiating sessions, in both formal and social settings. Very time-conscious foreign investors must recognize that time speaks with a Japanese accent—and that the common Western saying "time is of the essence" does not necessarily apply when doing business in Japan.

It is common practice in Japan for buyers and sellers to meet face-to-face and negotiate the purchase price and conditions in the presence of their real estate agents. Even in this case, attorneys are not usually present, and have traditionally been hired only when there is a need to file lawsuits or solve complex legal problems. Under normal circumstances, "judicial scriveners" *(shihoshoshi)* draft the necessary documents for all real estate transactions, including sales contracts and registration documents.

Despite the fact that many real estate transactions are conducted verbally, the Japanese real estate industry has been encouraging the use of listing contracts for the purpose of avoiding the misunderstandings that may arise from verbal agreements. The listing categories are exclusive right-to-sell listing *(senzoku baikai keiyaku)*, exclusive agency listing *(sennin baikai keiyaku)*, and open listing *(ippan baikai keiyaku)*. However, the terms and conditions of these contracts differ from those used in the United States.

The terms and conditions of the exclusive right-to-sell listing:

- Make one broker the sole and exclusive agent for the seller;
- Establish the period of the listing as three months or less, as stipulated by law;
- Prohibit the seller or sellers from selling the listed property on their own;
- Require the broker to register the listing with the REINS within five days of signing the contract;
- Require the broker to make a written report to the seller once a week or more;
- Allow the broker to obtain a proper commission, based on his contribution to the sale;
- Give the broker the right to ask for payment of a penalty and for expenses incurred if the seller violates the listing contract by selling the property on his own or by having another broker sell the property.

The terms and conditions of the exclusive agency listing contract:

- Make one broker the sole and exclusive agent for the seller;
- Establish the period of listing as three months or less, as stipulated by law;
- Allow the seller or sellers to sell the listed property on their own;

■ Require the broker to register the listing with the REINS within seven days of signing the contract;
■ Require the broker to make a written report to the seller once every two weeks or more;
■ Allow the broker to obtain a proper commission, based on his contribution to the sale;
■ Give the broker the right to ask for payment of a penalty and for expenses incurred if another broker sells the property within the listing period.

The terms and conditions of an open listing:
■ Allow the seller to list the same property with several brokers;
■ Define the standard period of listing as three months or less;
■ Allow the broker to obtain a proper commission, based on his contribution to the sale;
■ Allow the broker to ask for payment of expenses incurred if the property is sold by another broker.

The principal differences between the terms and conditions of Japanese listing contracts and American listing contracts are as follows: in Japan, (1) the length of the contract period is only three months, with three-month renewals possible; (2) the amount of sales commission is determined by the broker's contribution to the sale; (3) the broker can ask for payment of expenses incurred even under the open listing contract, if the seller succeeds in selling the property through another broker; and (4) the broker is entitled to receive a commission if the property sells during the contract period or within two years of the expiration date of the contract if the buyer was previously registered with the seller through the broker.

The maximum brokerage fee is 3 percent of the sales price. However, the same broker will often work for both the seller and the buyer, and thereby receive a double commission—3 percent from each party.

Real Estate Marketing Systems

Real estate marketing systems were developed by five major Japanese real estate companies as early as 1984. Despite the fact, however, that these companies agreed in principle to cooperate, full cooperation has not yet materialized. The largest marketing systems in major metropolitan areas are run by Mitsui Rehouse,

Nomura Residential Marketing Center, Odakyu Real Estate Associates, Tokyu Real Estate Group Network, and Towa Real Estate Center. Two large American real estate franchisers are also active in the Japanese market. In 1981, Electronic Realty Associates (ERA) joined with Mitsui Real Estate; in 1983, Century 21 entered into an agreement with Itochu Trading Company. Today, more than 250 Japanese real estate companies are franchisees of Century 21 Japan.

In 1998, to promote greater exchange of market information on real estate transactions, the MLIT established the Designated Marketing Network (Shitei Ryutsu Kiko), which is divided into four regions and has 37 locations nationwide. All of its members belong to the REINS.

- Higashi Nippon Fudosan Ryutsu Kiko, the East Japan REINS, covers Akita, Aomori, Chiba, Fukushima, Gunma, Hokkaido, Ibaraki, Iwate, Kanagawa, Miyagi, Nagano, Niigata, Saitama, Tochigi, Tokyo, Yamagata, and Yamanashi.
- Chubuken Fudosan Ryutsu Kiko, the Central District REINS, covers Aichi, Fukui, Gifu, Ishikawa, Mie, Shizuoka, and Toyama.
- Kinkiken Fudosan Ryutsu Kiko, or Kinki REINS, covers Hyogo, Kyoto, Nara, Osaka, Shiga, and Wakayama.
- Nishi Nippon Fudosan Ryutsu Kiko, the West Japan REINS, covers Ehime, Fukuoka, Hiroshima, Kagawa, Kagoshima, Kochi, Kumamoto, Miyazaki, Nagasaki, Oita, Okayama, Okinawa, Saga, Tokushima, Tottori, and Yamaguchi.

All members of the Designated Marketing Network must meet the following requirements:

- They must be bona fide members of either the Land and Building Brokers Association (Takuchi Tatemono Torihikigyo Kyokai), which exists in all 47 prefectures; the All-Japan Real Estate Association (Zen Nihon Fudosan Kyokai); the Real Estate Marketing Management Association (Fudosan Ryutsu Keiei Kyokai); or the Residential Industry Development Association (Jyutaku Sangyo Kaihatsu Kyokai).
- They must pay dues to support the operation of the marketing network.
- They are prohibited membership in the marketing network if they have had any record of reprimand or other major violation of the real estate transaction laws for the six months prior to becoming a member.
- They must have a computer system and facsimile machine suitable for exchanging information via the REINS.

A team approach is often taken by Japanese negotiators, who will want to reach consensus among themselves before responding to a proposal.

The members must report all sales activities more than once a week for properties on exclusive right-to-sell contracts, and more than once every two weeks for properties on exclusive-listing contracts. They are also required to register all sales of properties on exclusive right-to-sell contracts within five days, and to register all sales of properties on exclusive sales contracts within seven days after consummation.

The Context of Negotiations

In Japan, the negotiation process is quite different from that in other countries, and foreign investors—especially Americans—may find the differences frustrating to deal with. First of all, Japanese landowners have traditionally been accorded considerable status, and were able to demand very favorable terms when they sold their land. Thus, they are accustomed to deference from brokers—an attitude that has not been affected by the changes in the real estate market brought about by a prolonged recession. To make things more complex, a Japanese broker who does not actually have the exclusive right to sell a property may still try to represent the seller.

Second, there are at least three parties involved in the negotiation of a real estate transaction: the seller, the seller's bank representative, and the real estate broker. Because the transfer of certain types of land is subject to local government approval, a local government official may also be involved. For example, if more than four hectares (ten acres) of farmland are being transferred for development, approval is required from the Ministry of Agriculture, Forestry, and Fisheries.

Third, Japanese culture places a high value on saving face and avoiding personal confrontation; thus, negotiations in Japan tend to be more subtle and low-key than typical American negotiations.

In addition to these three factors, the foreign investor must consider two other important situational elements: the location of the negotiation, and the Japanese attitude toward time. The location of negotiating sessions has both practical and psychological implications. If the investor is in Japan, he has the advantage of being able to concentrate on the negotiations at hand, inspect the property, and obtain necessary information. However, the investor should not allow the fact that he is in a foreign country with different cultural traditions to give the sellers a psychological advantage. Japanese businesspeople are more than willing to spend large sums of money on entertaining. Although it is impolite and undiplomatic to flatly refuse an invitation, an investor should be wary of accepting lavish entertainment and thus being made to feel obligated. If possible, it is advisable to cancel out the obligation by countering with a similar invitation. For example, an investor might host a Western-style dinner party at his hotel in exchange for a local party hosted by the Japanese side.

Time is another critical factor. Highly time-conscious foreign investors must recognize that although "time is money" is a common saying even among Japanese businesspeople, in comparison to their Western counterparts they are very cautious, particularly when it comes to international business negotiations. Japanese sellers may use time to manipulate the negotiating process: for example, when the other side is pushing to consummate a deal by a certain deadline, Japanese sellers may intentionally delay a decision for no apparent reason, in order to obtain concessions. Such methods may sorely test the patience of foreign investors; indeed, many American businesspeople complain bitterly that the clock moves much more slowly in Japan.

Foreign investors should not tell their Japanese counterparts exactly when they are leaving (even if they want to rush them to meet their deadline), as this may be taken advantage of by the Japanese side. A longer stay also indicates a strong commitment, which will influence the Japanese negotiators' behavior during negotiating sessions.

A final important factor in negotiations is language. Even if all the Japanese negotiators appear to have a sufficient command of English, it is advisable for a foreign investor to hire his own interpreter for critical negotiating sessions. (If an investor asks the Japanese side to provide an interpreter, the interpreter probably would not be working for the investor's interest.) In order to avoid embarrassment, some Japanese negotiators may not admit that they cannot negotiate complex issues in English. An impartial professional interpreter will provide the investor with invaluable information, insights, and even important hints from nonverbal messages.

Unique Japanese Negotiating Tactics

Certain Japanese negotiating tactics might be considered unethical or otherwise unacceptable in the context of other countries' business practices. For example, Japanese negotiators routinely use padded offers when they do not know what to expect from foreign negotiators. They also use a tactic called *kama o kakeru,* which means "drawing out true intentions by making an outrageous offer." A foreign investor would be right to be suspicious if, after making a preposterous offer, the Japanese negotiators quickly changed it to a realistic one if they encountered a strong objection. Such tactics are in stark contrast to the typically more straightforward disclosure of information by American negotiators. The American approach—"You tell me what you want, and I'll tell you what we want"—will not work in Japan.

"You go first" is another tactic frequently used by Japanese negotiators. They typically will not disclose their own position without first knowing the opponents' position. The reason for this approach is that Japanese negotiators do not like to make themselves look foolish, and thereby lose face, by offering totally unacceptable requests.

Shifting the blame to the other side is another face-saving device that is often used by the Japanese side when difficult negotiations bog down. The Japanese believe strongly that they are honorable people, and this conviction may come into play during business negotiations: Japanese negotiators may accuse their opponents of insincerity, insisting that if they were sincere and willing to cooperate, all problems could be resolved.

Yet another Japanese negotiating tactic is the use of *amae*—indulgent dependency. When negotiating with a powerful opponent, it is not uncommon for Japanese negotiators to appeal to the opponent's generosity and to ask for understanding of their "desperate predicament." For example, the president of a bankrupt real estate company may try to humble himself, begging persistently to a rich investor. His intent is to make the investor feel guilty for keeping him in such a shameful and miserable state. Foreign investors may not necessarily encounter this particular tactic, but they should know that it is used in certain situations.

Initiating and Conducting Negotiations

In the United States, any large real estate transaction begins with a letter of intent, which is drafted by an attorney and is given to the seller by the buyer. In return, the seller gives the prospective buyer an agreement of confidentiality, which is drafted by his attorney. The letter of intent includes specific conditions of purchase, requests additional information, and specifies a period of time—known as the due diligence period—during which the buyer will research the property to be sold. In exchange for a certain amount of earnest money, the buyer retains exclusive right of purchase during the due diligence period.

Because many foreign investors, particularly Americans, are accustomed to using attorneys for real estate transactions, they are often accompanied by their attorney when they go to Japan to negotiate the purchase of property. But in Japan, investors and real estate agents almost never ask their attorneys to be present at the beginning of business discussions, and the attorneys of foreign investors will not normally be welcome.

Opening the initial negotiating session with Japanese negotiators requires a few important social rituals. First, Japanese negotiators need to establish amicable social relations and a pleasant atmosphere before getting down to business. Ten or 20 minutes will be spent drinking tea or coffee, introducing each member of the Japanese team, and inquiring about the opponents' personal backgrounds, hobbies, and interests. Second, during this period, one or two top Japanese executives may appear for five or ten minutes, just for *aisatsu* (greeting), and to have a cup of tea with the foreign visitors. However, these executives do not usually participate in the actual negotiations: their function is mainly ceremonial, and they are there only for the exchange of business cards *(meishi)*.

In discussing agenda items, Japanese negotiators usually take a holistic or nonsequential approach; that is, they do not necessarily address agenda items one at a time, and in order. American negotiators are often disturbed by what they perceive as "conversational meandering" because, in the United States, they are used to settling issues in a logical sequence. They must play along with the Japanese, however, by being patient and accepting their ways. For example, if one of the Japanese negotiators brings up an issue that the American side thought was already agreed upon, it is not a good idea to say, "I thought we covered that point already. Did you change your mind again?" This kind of statement causes the Japanese negotiator to lose face.

American negotiators are fond of arguing logically about everything, as they have been taught to defend their contentions by asserting themselves. Even though their arguments may be supported flawlessly by appropriate data, the Japanese will be skeptical of such an approach. In Japan, a reputation for being "overly logical" undermines a negotiator's reputation for integrity and trustworthiness because the Japanese are averse to aggressive logical attacks. In Japan, polite persuasion works much better than American-style logical argument. Americans also need to be aware that they can easily overwhelm the Japanese by dominating the verbal interaction while the Japanese show little physical or verbal activity.

Foreign negotiators must recognize that the Japanese negotiators may need extra time to respond to questions in English. More importantly, no member of the Japanese negotiating team will speak up and disclose a personal opinion, and the members of the Japanese negotiating team will have little or no authority to make on-the-spot decisions. A negotiator who is forced to respond immediately will engage in private conversations in Japanese at the conference table, or may remain silent for a long time. In some instances the negotiator may even say "Yes"—which does not really mean yes, but is designed to get beyond a difficult situation.

Foreign investors need to develop flexible communication strategies to cope with possible conflicts and to look for signposts indicating "give points" and "must points." Their offers and counteroffers must be based on prior fact-finding research and informal consultations *(nemawashi)*. They cannot just read the Japanese government statistics, trade journals, and real estate news printed in English and come up with an initial offer. They need to go to several different sources and talk to both Japanese and foreign businesspeople who are sufficiently familiar with the most recent real estate transactions. In many cases, Japanese businesspeople offer "confidential information," verbally and off the record (called *ofureko* in Japanese), which can be very valuable. For their part, foreign investors should also be prepared to provide give points—trade-offs that allow accommodation to the Japanese side.

Coping with Frustrations at the Negotiating Table

Many problems at the negotiating table emerge from contrasting negotiating styles, differences in business practices, and differences in social customs. The most serious problem is that American negotiators must cope with a much slower style of bargaining in Japan. This does not mean that Japanese negotiators are not conscious of time and deadlines, but it does mean that they want to be cautious and thorough. They are not used to signing a lengthy contract with a lot of contingencies when they make a deal. They will take a team approach, and will want to reach a consensus among themselves before responding to anything. In addition, they may have to talk to their creditors and local government officials and ask for their concurrence or approval.

Another cause of frustration is that the members of the Japanese negotiating team usually have little or no authority to make on-the-spot decisions. In Japan, all major decisions are made through *ringi*—group decision making. Furthermore, Japanese negotiators are usually not given authority to make even minor concessions that have not been discussed prior to negotiation. They abhor taking personal risks to expedite the decision-making process, especially when it comes to negotiating multimillion-dollar deals. In fact, even the chief Japanese negotiator will hesitate to make decisions on his own unless he is the founder and the majority shareholder of the company he represents.

It is necessary to know who the real decision maker is and not to assume that the Japanese representatives have enough authority and responsibility to consummate a deal. In other words, the foreign investors must realize that they are negotiating not only with those Japanese negotiators across the conference table but also with their colleagues and superiors at the head office.

Some Japanese nonverbal behaviors are puzzling to businesspeople from other cultures. The Japanese are trained to put on an impassive or stoic face in formal situations. They almost never smile at strangers, and usually look away when they have accidental eye contact. In Western culture, sustained eye contact indicates that people are interested, honest, and positive. In Japanese culture, however, the same sustained eye contact could mean aggression, rudeness, insistence on equality, and even belligerence. Lack of good eye contact may make negotiation difficult for some American negotiators.

Japanese smiles and laughter carry more than universal meanings of happiness, joy, or agreement. One such example is the smile of embarrassment, which means, "I'm sorry. I don't understand what you are saying. You are speaking so fast." Another example is the laughter of contempt, which means, "You must be kidding. How could you make such a stupid demand!"

After the Negotiation

Once verbal agreements are reached, it is time to start working on a written contract. In the American business context, the exact wording of terms and conditions is of absolute importance. In the Japanese business context, however, establishing solid personal relationships with each member of the opposing negotiating team is far more important. This does not imply that Japanese businesspeople ignore a written contract, but that they have a different

Foreign investors need to be aware that negotiating sessions in Japan require important social rituals, such as establishing a relaxed atmosphere before getting down to business. After a major deal is concluded, a formal signing ceremony is typically held.

approach to its implementation. Although this attitude is gradually changing, many will sign a contract without having their attorneys review it because they assume that the rights and duties of the contract are provisional or tentative, rather than absolute. They believe that the specific items of a contract are open to renegotiation whenever economic circumstances change drastically.

To avoid contractual disputes in Japan, two things are imperative: the contract must be in both English and Japanese, and it must be written by bilingual attorneys who are familiar with both American and Japanese laws. The attorneys must explain every important clause and ensure that it is fully understood by the Japanese side. If possible, it is wise to include a clause stating that in case of a contractual dispute, the English contract takes precedence over the Japanese translation of the original contract, and that the location of the court of appeal will be in the United States.

Ceremonies and celebrations are an important aspect of Japanese business culture. Japanese companies hold a formal signing ceremony when sealing a major business deal. American companies may consider such an event a waste of time and money, but it is a good public relations opportunity: guests of honor and other invitees will include local politicians, government officials, officials of trade organizations, and television and newspaper reporters. During the signing ceremony, the top executives of both sides publicly sign the contract, congratulatory speeches are made, and commemorative gifts are exchanged. At the elaborate cocktail party that follows, all the participants will mingle and socialize, and news reporters will interview the top executives.

Conflict Resolution

Under American business practices, contractual disputes are almost always handled by attorneys and settled in court. Japanese businesspeople prefer to settle their disputes through mutual consultation *(hanashiai)*, mediation *(chukai)*, and arbitration *(chusai)*, without going to court. Japanese businesspeople rarely sue each other because their business relationships have traditionally been personal and subjective. Generally, the Japanese find litigation distasteful and destructive. They would rather compromise and settle out of court to avoid the public embarrassment and bad publicity of a long legal battle.

A recommended way to resolve a legal dispute in Japan is to go through consultation at the staff members' level, without involving any executives. Only after the staff members have come up with a few mutually acceptable solutions will they consult the top executives for advice and endorsement of the best alternative. If informal consultations do not work, a mediator needs to be hired to help resolve the dispute. The mediator may be the *shokaisha*—the person who originally introduced the two parties—or it may be someone who has many years of experience in international business. Arbitration is an alternative, but it is difficult to find a competent arbitrator in Japan.

Under current circumstances, it is a mistake to assume that American business laws can be applied to international business disputes in Japan. The best advice to foreign investors is to avoid filing lawsuits and to use the Japanese approach of solving contractual disputes through cooperation and compromise.

Chapter 3

Assessing Market Value

There are a variety of resources and methods that buyers can use to determine the market value of real property in Japan. Government-sponsored appraisals, undertaken annually, can provide useful reference points for buyers and can supplement other methods of determining market value, including the cost approach, the market-comparison approach, and the income approach.

Japanese Appraisers

Japanese real estate appraisers are members of the Japanese Association of Real Estate Appraisers, the only professional association of appraisers in Japan. Established in 1965, the association has a membership of about 5,500 licensed appraisers and is under the control of the Ministry of Land, Infrastructure, and Transport (MLIT). The objectives of the association are

- To maintain the dignity of licensed real estate appraisers *(fudosan kanteishi)* and licensed assistant real estate appraisers *(fudosan kanteishiho)* and to improve their standing;
- To strive constantly for the progress and improvement of real estate appraisal work;
- To contribute to the development of the real estate appraisal system and sustain the formulation of appropriate pricing of land.

Because appraisers must go through years of apprenticeship and then pass a series of rigorous examinations to be licensed by the MLIT, appraisers are in short supply. Japan's depressed real estate market—and the resulting sudden influx of foreign investors—has also created a strong demand for appraisers.

Many Japanese real estate appraisers are independent professional appraisers and owners of small or medium-sized appraisal companies. They perform work for private financial institutions; real estate companies; individual buyers or sellers of property; and national, regional, and local governments. Their work for government clients includes

- Land-price surveys of representative plots of land that are commissioned by the central government in accordance with the National Land Use Planning Act.
- Land-price surveys of representative plots of land that are commissioned by the prefectural governments. Such surveys may include detailed research on price fluctuations in designated areas to determine whether prices in those areas should continue to be monitored.
- Land-price surveys of representative plots of land designated for inheritance and gift taxation by the National Tax Agency.
- Property tax assessments commissioned by cities, towns, and villages.

Government-Sponsored Appraisals and Other Indicators of Value

There are three government-sponsored appraisals: posted price *(koji kakaku)*, standard price *(kijun kakaku)*, and roadside price *(rosenka)*. The appraisal for posted price is a nationwide appraisal of a large variety of land parcels—some 31,000 sites—designated by the MLIT; the land prices are as of January 1, and the results are released in late March. The posted price is used by the

FIGURE 3-1

Posted Price and Standard Price, Ginza Area

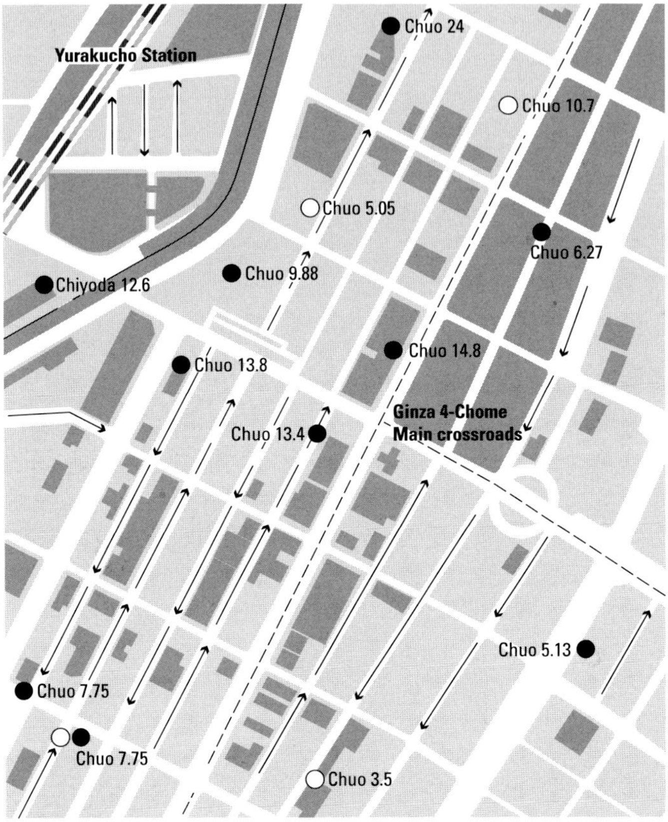

● Posted price
○ Standard price

Note: Numbers represent millions of yen per square meter

government as a guideline for real estate transactions and the acquisition of land for public use.

The appraisal for standard price is commissioned by municipal governments and is conducted annually on some 28,000 sites, which generally do not include those sites used for the survey of posted prices. The land prices are as of July 1, and the results are released in the middle of September each year. The purpose of the survey is to help municipal government agencies regulate and implement the rules and regulations of real estate transactions, but it also provides supplementary data to the posted price.

The valuation of roadside prices *(rosenka)* is conducted on most major roads in urban areas throughout Japan every year. It is commissioned by the National Tax Agency for the purpose of determining the roadside land appraisal value of roadside properties and is used to calculate the bases for inheritance and gift taxes. In an approach that is unique from an American perspective, the roadside price is assigned to roads, and not to individual properties. Taking January 1 as the appraisal date, the National Tax Agency determines roadside

FIGURE 3-2

Roadside Price, Ginza Area, 2002

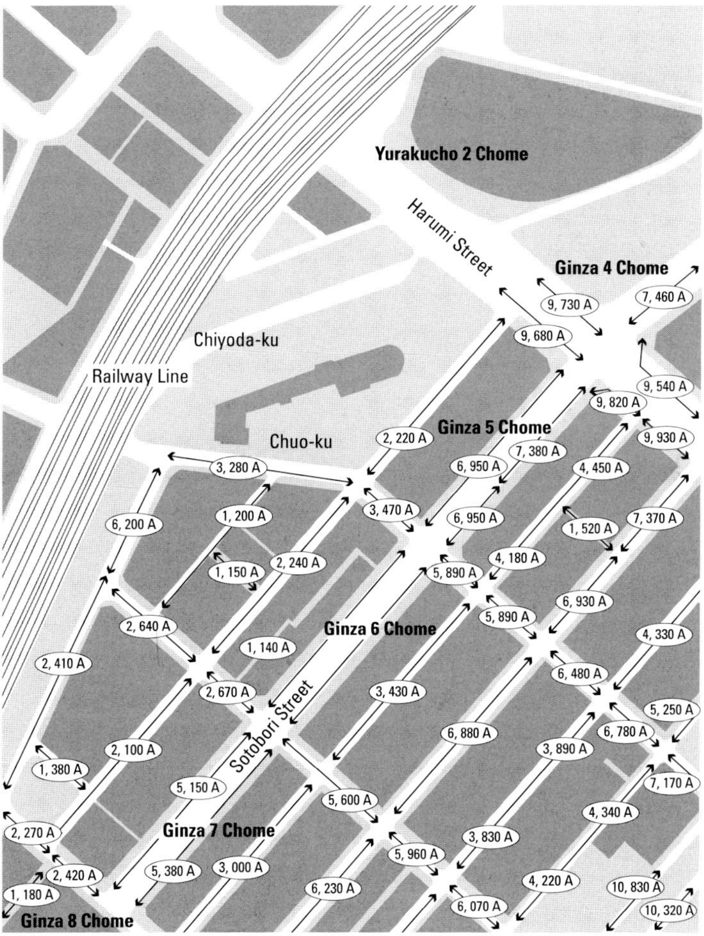

Note: Numbers represent thousands of yen per square meter.

prices on the basis of consultations with experts in the real estate industry and with reference to published posted prices, past real estate transaction prices, and appraisal prices prepared by real estate appraisers. The roadside price, expressed as the yen-per-square-meter value of the road, is set at approximately 80 percent of the posted price.

Land with greater frontage generally has a higher value, as it can be used more efficiently. For the same reason, a parcel of land that is regularly shaped and generally well proportioned has a higher value. These factors are important for determining the value of a piece of property using the "roadside land appraisal method" *(rosenkahoushiki ni yoru hyoka)*. The formula to determine

FIGURE 3-3

Using Roadside Price to Calculate Roadside Land Appraisal Value

Roadside land appraisal value = roadside price x land area x site coefficient.

The site coefficient is calculated by taking into account the shape of the site, the width of the site's frontage, and the ratio of frontage to the depth of the site.

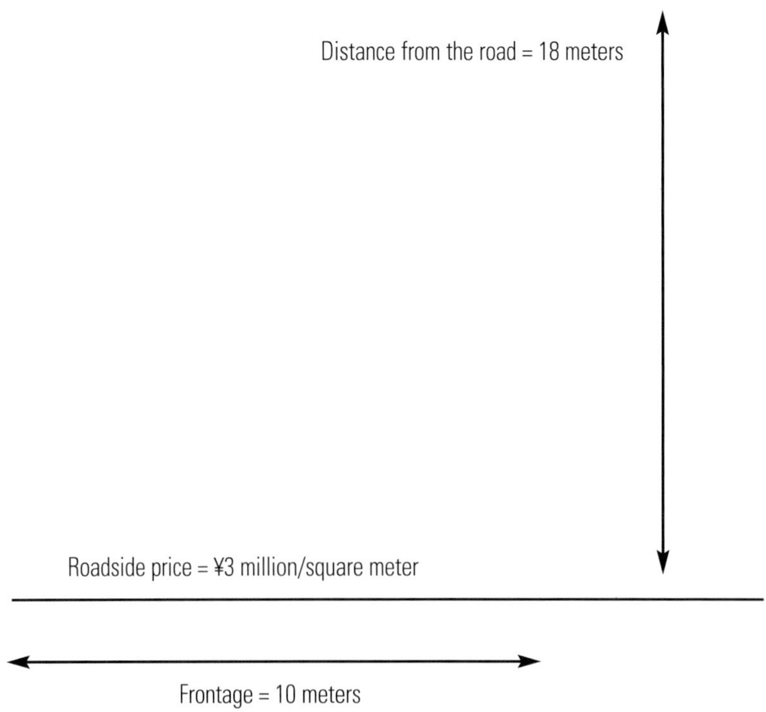

the "roadside land appraisal value" is as follows: Roadside land appraisal value = roadside price x land area x site coefficient.

Each site has its own conditions, which must be accounted for in determining the value of the land, and these are reflected in the site coefficient. The site coefficient takes into account the shape of the site, the width of the frontage, and the ratio of frontage to the distance between the site and the road. The maximum site coefficient is 1.

Consider, for example, a parcel of land that has 10 meters (33 feet) of frontage, is 18 meters (59 feet) from the road, has been assigned a roadside price of ¥3 million per square meter ($2,534 per square foot), and has an assumed site coefficient of 1 (see figure 3-3). The roadside land appraisal value would be ¥3,000,000 x 10 meters x 18 meters x 1 = ¥540,000,000 ($2,534 x 33 feet x 59 feet x 1 = $4,933,698).

While not publicly announced, the appraisal for the fixed-asset tax *(koteishisan zei)* is commissioned by the city, town, or village government and is conducted at 415,000 sites every three years. The purpose of the appraisal is to determine the benchmark land price for property tax assessment and the registration stamp tax,

One of the most exclusive and expensive shopping areas in Japan, Tokyo's Ginza district is home to some of the world's most prominent luxury retailers. Property in Ginza is among the most expensive in the city.

a tax paid at the time a property is registered. The appraisal for the fixed-asset tax is approximately 70 percent of the posted price.

Other land-price indicators include the following:

- The Urban Land-Price Index, published biannually by the Japan Real Estate Institute and based on the institute's research on six indices in 223 cities, including the six major cities of Kobe, Kyoto, Nagoya, Osaka, Tokyo, and Yokohama;
- The Short-Term Land-Price Trends Survey (Tanki Chika Doko Chosa), conducted quarterly by the National Land Agency at 949 sites (582 residential and 367 commercial) nationwide and focusing on percentage change in the posted price and standard price;
- The Nikkei Office Rent Survey, a biannual survey of office rental fees undertaken by the Nippon Keizai Shimbun in 23 major cities nationwide.

Appraisal Issues

Japanese appraisers need to contend with unique factors that may influence their appraisal process and final report. Since there is no industrywide multiple listing system in Japan, appraisers do not have reliable statistical data on listing prices and sales prices for property transactions. Moreover, sales prices may not be available even in the records of local registry offices. Office rental prices listed in the publications of leasing companies are *kibo chintairyo*—"offering rents"—not actual rents: actual rents are often kept confidential between the lessor and the lessee. (See chapter 5 for a more detailed discussion of office leasing.) Appraisers usually rely on records of government appraisals (which are publicly available) and on informal channels to gather reliable information.

In reading any appraisal report on a Japanese property, foreign investors need to pay special attention to two important factors. First, because of the traditional Japanese land-valuation method, the land value is comparatively higher than that of buildings and other improvements. Second, there are few large parcels of land, and many properties are a collection of several parcels of land. (A lot under a large office building or a condominium may even be a combination of freehold and leasehold land parcels.)

Foreign investors also need to be aware that in Japan, the appraisal fee is based on a percentage of the appraised value, while in the United States it is usually based on how many hours the appraisal took and what expenses were incurred.

Categories of Appraisal Prices

In Japan, real property is assigned four different appraisal prices:

■ Regular price *(seijo kakaku)* is the marketable price of a real property under normal market conditions.

■ Special price *(gentei kakaku)* is the price when a certain limitation is imposed; for example, if the value of Parcel A increases when it is combined with Parcel B, then part of Parcel A should be included in the appraisal price of Parcel B, and this "special" appraisal price is called *gentei kakaku*.

■ Specified price *(tokutei kakaku)* is the appraisal price for a real property that has been used for collateral in a nonperforming loan.

■ Specific price *(tokushu kakaku)* is the price of real property that is not marketable to ordinary buyers. (An example of a specific price might be that assigned to a historic building with relatively little economic value.)

In the United States, property values are generally classified as market value, assessed value, loan value, insurance value, leased fee-value, and plottage value. Market value is an estimate based on the highest price a buyer would be willing—but not compelled—to pay, and the lowest price that a seller—who is willing, but not compelled, to sell—would accept. Assessed value is the value used for property tax purposes. Book value is the value at which an asset is carried on a balance sheet; it is the cost of the asset minus accumulated depreciation. Loan value is the value as established by a lender for loan purposes. Insurance value is the value based on the cost of reproduction, replacement, or reimbursement for loss of the property. Leased fee-value is the value of the landlord's rights to the property being leased. Plottage value is the increased value produced by combining smaller, individually owned lots into a larger tract under single ownership.

With regard to the assessment of property value, one important difference between Japan and the United States concerns leasehold *(chinshakuken)* value. In Japan, the rights of lessees are much stronger than they are in many other countries because they are protected by lease laws and age-old practices. For example, even after a lease contract has expired, a lessor cannot evict a lessee without a compelling reason. A lessor who does so will have to pay a large sum of "eviction compensation" *(tachinoki ryo)*, which can be between 30 and 70 percent of the value of a leased land, depending on the terms negotiated. However, as mentioned in chapter 1, landlords are now offering investors more flexible options in this regard because of Japan's weak economic climate. (See chapter 5 for more a detailed discussion of lease laws.)

Factors That Affect Appraisals

In appraisal, it is necessary to consider carefully four elements of real property value: utility, scarcity, demand, and transferability. Utility is the power to render a service or fill a need. If a property has no use, it will have no value. Scarcity is determined by the relationship between supply and demand. In Japan, this element is critical because of the chronic scarcity of developable land. Demand comes from the existence of a need and the monetary power to satisfy that need. Today, many Japanese real properties are still in demand, but are not marketable because of the difficulty of obtaining financing. Transferability refers to ownership and to possession and control of the rights of ownership. If a property is not transferable, it has very little value even if utility, scarcity, and demand are present.

Other economic principles that are important to the appraisal process are the principle of highest and best use, the principle of conformity, and the principle of anticipation. Highest and best use refers to the utilization of real property to its greatest economic advantage: that is, the use provides the highest possible land value and net income stream. Conformity refers to the extent to which the use of a real property and its improvements blend in with the surroundings. It may also refer to social and economic uniformity. Zoning regulations and private deed restrictions discourage the mixed use of land and promote reasonable uniformity.

Anticipation refers to all present and future benefits expected from the ownership and use of real property. Before and during the bubble economy, when property values were skyrocketing, Japanese investors relied too much on the principle of anticipation in forecasting property values. Now, however, the same principle is being used to create extremely negative forecasts of property values.

It is also important to consider four more elements that influence property value: social, physical, economic, and governmental considerations. Social considerations include prestige, safety and security, and demographic characteristics (e.g., family size, social and economic factors) associated with a particular property and its environment. In Tokyo, for example, the prestigious locations for offices are Marunouchi, Roppongi, Shibuya, Shinbashi, and Shinjuku, which

Often compared to Paris's Champs-Elysées, the Omotesando district is a haven for trendy shoppers. Many foreign luxury retailers have built large-scale flagship stores there, and property prices have been rising swiftly.

house modern, high-rise office buildings occupied by leading multinational corporations, financial institutions, and government agencies. The prestigious residential areas are Aoyama, Akasaka, Azabu, Roppongi, Shirogane, and Takanawa; these districts, where wealthy foreigners and Japanese people live in high-priced single-family residences and deluxe condominiums, have good security and are considered desirable social environments.

Physical considerations might include street patterns and width, and access to public transportation, schools, shopping, parks, recreational facilities, and houses of worship. Physical features such as the shape and size of a lot, and its location in relation to the city center, are also very important, especially for residential properties.

Because Japanese roads are extremely congested and automobile access is very difficult in metropolitan centers, foreign investors need to pay particularly close attention to a site's access to subways, trains, and major highways. They also need to be aware of local building codes and zoning regulations, especially if they intend to rebuild or to add to an existing building. The neighborhood's attitude toward what might be built must also be considered

Economic considerations might include rent levels, vacancy rates, residents' income levels, amount of nearby new construction, amount of nearby vacant land, and neighborhood growth patterns. Rent levels, vacancy rates, and the level of new office construction in the area can be particularly important in the appraisal of office buildings.

Governmental considerations include laws and taxation, zoning and building codes, and other governmental regulations that affect the value of real property. National, prefectural, and local governments in Japan levy several different real property taxes; in addition, they impose strict regulations on the construction of improvements. Foreign investors need to be aware of local building codes and zoning regulations, especially if they intend to rebuild or to add to an existing building.

Appraisal Methods

Japanese appraisers use the cost approach, the market-comparison approach, and the income approach to conduct appraisals. But these methods are not applied in the same way as they are in America—first because the methods are influenced by traditional Japanese appraisal concepts, and second because Japanese appraisals are still being affected by the sky-high real property values that were in effect before the bursting of the bubble economy. Appraisers will choose the most suitable appraisal method from among the most common methods. The following sections describe the three principal methods.

Cost Approach

Until recently, the cost approach was the method given highest priority by Japanese appraisers because it was considered the most appropriate method during the years that land prices were increasing by leaps and bounds. However, now that many real properties in Japan are valued below their replacement cost, it may no longer be appropriate to use the cost approach alone.

The principal advantage of the cost approach is that it can be used to establish the upper limit of the cost of replacing a building; the principal disadvantage is that the cost of replacing a building does not always indicate its true value. In fact, there may be a considerable difference between the cost of replacing a building and that building's value in the open market. Another disadvantage arises in the case of older buildings: because depreciation cannot be precisely measured, their replacement cost is difficult to estimate accurately.

The cost approach consists of four basic steps:

1. Estimate the value of the land.
2. Estimate the current cost of replacing the building.
3. Estimate and deduct the amount of depreciation.
4. Add the estimated land value to the depreciated reproduction or replacement cost of the building: this yields the total value of the property.

Estimate Land Value. If the land has been developed recently, the value is the sum of the original land price plus the development cost. If not, the value is estimated on the basis of comparisons with similar properties that have been developed recently.

Estimate Replacement Cost. In Japan, the replacement cost—the total cost of constructing a similar building, delivered to its owner in turnkey condition—can be derived in one of two ways: in the direct method, total construction cost is derived by summing direct construction costs, indirect construction costs, profit for the contractor, and other expenses. The indirect method compares estimates of the construction costs for similar buildings to a rough estimate of the replacement cost of the subject property. In the United States, the cost estimate is per square foot or per cubic foot, while in Japan the estimate is per square meter.

The four common approaches to estimating replacement cost used in the United States are the quantity-survey method, the unit-cost-in-place method, the cubic-foot method, and the square-foot method. The quantity-survey method (also called the contractor's method) arrives at a replacement cost by taking account of the quantity and grade of each material used and the total hours of labor required. In the unit-cost-in-place method, the estimate of replacement cost is derived from the cost of labor and materials for each component part of the building, such as the foundation, roof, floor, walls, and fixtures. In the cubic-foot method, the outside of the building is measured to determine the total volume of the building, and the cost per cubic foot is applied to the total number of cubic feet. The square-foot method is analogous to the cubic-foot method, except that the per-square-foot cost of all components is multiplied by the total floor area.

Estimate Depreciation. The three principal categories of depreciation are deterioration, functional obsolescence, and external obsolescence, which are further broken down into curable (replacement, repair, or correction is economically feasible) and incurable (correction is not economically feasible). There are two ways to calculate depreciation: one is to determine the number of durable years of the building, which is derived from the building's type (e.g., office, retail, residential) and structure (e.g., wood, steel, reinforced concrete), as stipulated by Japanese accounting rules; the other method is to examine the building on site and to check the deterioration of each part of the building.

Market-Comparison Approach

The market-comparison approach (also known as the market-data approach or the direct sales comparison approach) is considered the most reliable gauge of the market and is most frequently used to appraise residential properties. However, this approach requires an active real estate market for the type of property being appraised. In the market-comparison approach, the value of a given property is determined by comparing the prices actually paid for similar properties. For a property to be considered similar, it must have the same highest and best use as the subject property and be reasonably comparable in size, location, physical condition, and other such characteristics. In addition, the comparative sales must have occurred recently (within the past three months). (Properties sold through bankruptcy or foreclosure, properties sold by the government, and properties transferred between relatives or related companies should be excluded from this method because the sales prices of these properties do not reflect normal market conditions.)

There are three main steps in the market-comparison approach:

1. Locate several comparable properties.
2. Compare the selected properties with the subject property and make any necessary adjustments in the sales prices to account for any significant differences in age, location, or physical characteristics.
3. Reconcile all the comparable information and draw a conclusion of value.

Locate Comparable Properties. An appraiser must carefully check each of the comparable properties by reviewing Japanese government statistics; the official sales records of the Real Estate Information Network System (REINS); and other reliable sources. As noted earlier, it is extremely difficult to find the actual

The Shibuya district, which has several large department stores, is one of the most popular shopping and entertainment areas in Tokyo. Shown here is the famous Hachiko crossing at Shibuya Station, one of the busiest crossings in the world. Over 2 million people pass through Shibuya Station each day.

sales prices of properties and related information in Japan. Sales information is not open to the public, and the official records of title transfers in local registry offices do not include sales prices. Nor is the amount of stamp duty paid a good indication of the price of a large real estate transaction, since the maximum amount of stamp duty is ¥540,000 ($4,990).

Compare Properties and Make Adjustments. In comparing properties, appraisers make adjustments even in the case of vacant land because lots may differ in topography, location, and utility hookups. Adjustments must also be made to compare apartment buildings: there may be differences in the number of units, the size of the lot, the age of the building, the style, the number of parking spaces, the physical condition, and the number of bedrooms and bathrooms in each unit.

Reconcile Information and Assign a Value. A final check of the data is undertaken and the information is used by the appraiser to assign a value to the property.

Income Approach

In the income approach, the market value of a property is the present worth of the projected future income stream over the property's remaining economic life. In other words, an income-producing property is worth what a buyer will pay for it in order to have the right to receive the income. In Japan, the income approach is now widely used by both domestic and foreign firms, particularly as project financing becomes more common. During the bubble economy, however, Japanese appraisers rarely stressed the income approach because land prices were skyrocketing every month, and banks were financing more than 100 percent of land value—so there was no concern about future income streams. Japanese companies and even individual investors were buying up almost everything for quick profits. During this period, the Japanese government levied special taxes to curb the runaway inflation of land values.

There are four basic steps in the income approach:

1. Estimate potential gross income.
2. Estimate effective gross income.
3. Deduct annual operating expenses to arrive at net income.
4. Estimate the capitalization rate and property value.

Estimate Potential Gross Income. Gross income refers to the total annual income the subject property would be likely to produce if it were fully occupied. In determining the potential gross income of a building, an appraiser must consider the type of rent involved. Economic rent is the rent that the property would command if it were vacant and available for rent in the open market. Contract rent is the rent that current tenants are paying. The appraiser must also look at the "quality" of the income, which refers to the financial responsibility of the tenants, and the "durability" of the income, which refers to the remaining length of time the income stream will continue.

As noted earlier, it is difficult to obtain reliable statistics on actual rents and lease terms in Japan because property management companies and building owners usually give out offering rents *(kibo chintairyo),* which do not reflect actual rents. In addition, there are many instances in which the building owner's company and the tenants belong to the same *keiretsu* (*keiretsu* are groups of large business enterprises). In these cases, lease contracts are usually one or two years in length, with an implicit understanding that they will be automatically renewed.

Estimate Effective Gross Income. Effective gross income is the potential gross income less an allowance for vacancy, loss from bad debts, and collection expenses.

Deduct Operating Expenses to Arrive at Net Income. Operating expenses include the following:

- Fixed expenses: those expenses, such as real property taxes and insurance, that remain the same whether or not the units are rented;
- Expenses such as management fees, utilities, advertising, interior and exterior maintenance, janitorial service, security service, and grounds care;
- Reserve funds for the replacement of equipment and building components such as stoves, refrigerators, air conditioners, carpets, drapes, and water heaters.

Estimate the Capitalization Rate and Property Value. It should be noted that in determining the appropriate capitalization rate on the annual net income, principal or interest payments on existing mortgages and income tax on the return on the investment are not deductible as operating expenses but as applied expenses. Investors and appraisers use the capitalization rate to determine the value of an income property in a specific market: the value of a given property is the annual net income (or an average of several years), divided by the capitalization rate. The capitalization rate, in turn, is the sum of the discount rate and the recapture rate. The discount rate is a compound interest rate used to convert expected future income into a present value. The recapture rate is the rate of recovery of an investment in a wasting asset (an asset that diminishes in value over time). For example, a building with a 50-year estimated useful life has a recapture rate of 2 percent.

If the estimated net income of a building is ¥10,000 per year, and an appraiser selects a capitalization rate of 10 percent (a discount rate—return on investment—of 8 percent and a recapture rate of 2 percent), then the estimated value of the building will be ¥100,000 (¥10,000/0.10 = ¥100,000.) Capitalization rates are usually developed by analyzing the selling price, gross income, and operating expenses for comparable properties in a given marketplace. The rate that prevails in a particular marketplace is usually called the market cap rate. Where data on comparable properties are not available, appraisers will construct a capitalization rate.

Determination of the appropriate capitalization rate is also influenced by the conditions under which the particular investment is being operated and by prevailing interest rates, the availability of funds, and risks. Since the building has a limited productive life, the investor also needs to make provision, in his analysis, for using depreciation before the end of the building's economic life.

Traditionally, American investors have found it difficult to find investments in Japan that provided a high capitalization rate (5 to 8 percent) because Japanese investors were often content with a much lower rate (2 to 3 percent). These days, however, Japanese institutional investors are demanding higher rates. For example, according to a survey conducted by the Japan Real Estate Institute (Nihon Fudosan Kenkyujo) in October 2003, developers, financial institutions, and financial investors in Japan were anticipating rates of 5 to 8 percent: 5.2 percent for Class A office space; 6 to 6.5 percent for residential buildings in the Tokyo metropolis; 5 to 5.6 percent for high-end specialty retail stores in prime locations, such as Ginza and Omotesando; and 8 percent for suburban shopping centers.

In the case of an income property, an appraiser can usually make a separate determination of the land value (by using comparables) and of the building value (by using replacement cost), once the overall market value of the property has been derived using the income approach. It is possible to use a residual appraisal technique to determine the value of the land or the buildings independently. The land-residual approach subtracts the value of the buildings from the overall value of the property, taking the remainder as the value of the land. Building values may be estimated on the basis of their replacement cost or depreciated value. The building-residual approach arrives at a value for land, then treats the difference between the overall property value and the land value as the building's value. Land values may be estimated by comparison to other land parcels in the same area. The higher the land value in relation to the overall property value, the lower the building value—and vice versa.

Chapter 4

Land Use and Building Regulations

In all real estate transactions, a thorough understanding of zoning ordinances, building codes, and other applicable restrictions is essential. This is particularly true in Japan because many older commercial buildings, hotels, residential condominiums, houses, and other structures predate current land use and building regulations. But because of changes in regulations that have occurred since these structures were built, certain land parcels and subdivisions cannot be developed or redeveloped. The recent regulations may not only affect the permitted use but may also negatively affect the value of these real properties.

Land use ordinances in Japan are influenced by the scarcity of developable land and by the country's large population. In addition, strict building regulations have been adopted to cope with the natural disasters to which Japan is subject, which include earthquakes, tidal waves, and typhoons. Both zoning and building codes are enforced by the Building Standards Law at the national, prefectural, and local levels.

Special Administrative Agencies are tasked with enforcing zoning and building codes under the Building Standards Law. Prefectural governments; the governments of cities with populations of over 250,000; and the governments of some smaller cities, which have negotiated the rights with the prefectural government, are eligible to become Special Administrative Agencies. (The governments of most Japanese cities with over 100,000 residents are designated as Special Administrative Agencies.) The prefectural governor or city mayor, as head of the jurisdictional government, is granted the right to issue building permits and other related licenses.

In addition, for the 23 wards in Tokyo and other densely populated cities that need special attention, the ward government is designated the Special Administrative Agency. At the ward level, the right to issue building permits and other related licenses is invested in the ward mayor. Although the Building Standards Law is a single, national law, ordinances at lower levels of government are supplementary to it and consonant with it.

The City Planning Law, promulgated in 1968, applies to urban and urbanizing areas (known as City Planning Areas) that may encompass several administrative units. Among the law's objectives are:

- To regulate and guide land use through the Land Development Permission System;
- To clarify the responsibilities of the public and private sectors in sharing costs for public facilities;
- To promote the development and improvement of public facilities;
- To introduce democratic processes to city planning;
- To devolve regulatory powers to the local level.

The law covers, among other areas, land use control, the planning of public facilities, the development of district plans, and city planning procedures.

Although Japanese building codes and zoning ordinances may seem rigid at first glance, they are generally open to interpretation in some matters. It is helpful to have access to a local professional (for example, a general contractor or architect) who has experience with, and fully understands, land use and building regulations. Such professionals can discuss the regulations with local authorities to ensure that the codes are interpreted correctly.

The Building Standards Law

The purpose of the Building Standards Law, enacted in 1950, is to protect life and property from natural disasters and to protect public health by ensuring high environmental standards. Although the law applies to buildings throughout Japan, it allows room for different standards within each region. The law includes general provisions (administrative, miscellaneous, and penalties associated with infractions); building codes (structural, fire safety, and hygienic safety); and zoning codes (relation between building sites and roads; land use and zoning regulations; building height, bulk, and shape controls; and restrictions that apply to fire-protection districts).

The Building Standards Law specifies structural safety standards to safeguard against seismic tremors from earthquakes, snow load from heavy snowfalls, wind pressure from typhoons, and other predictable natural phenomena. It also specifies the required structural strength, quality, and safety of structural materials; technical standards for construction methods; and structural calculations. The fire-safety standards under the Building Standards Law are designed to prevent the outbreak and spread of fire within buildings and the spread of fire from one building to another.

Under city regulations, building heights in Osaka's Midosuji district were once heavily restricted. The regulations have since changed, but one can see that on this block, most buildings are still exactly the same height.

Foreign investors considering purchasing existing buildings or developing new projects in Japan must carefully evaluate the extent to which buildings or proposed buildings meet safety requirements. Although the Building Standards Law establishes minimum standards, it is still prudent for a purchaser to inspect the structure to determine whether the building has met those standards. If the building has been renovated, the standard of the renovations needs to be checked. Finally, since the laws change with time, many older buildings are not up to code. The age of the building is very important if an older structure is being purchased.

The Building Standards Law is constantly being updated and revised to reflect changing conditions. In 2003, for example, in response to an increase in sick-building syndrome (health problems caused by volatile chemical substances contained in building materials), the Japanese government revised the Building Standards Law to limit the use of chemical substances such as formaldehyde and chlorpyrifos.

Zoning

The zoning codes of most U.S. communities provide detailed specifications describing permitted uses within designated areas. For example, the *Highlights of the Comprehensive Zoning Code of the City and County of Honolulu* lists seven residential districts (from estate residential to urban residential); for each district, the code provides specific, straightforward information describing permitted principal uses; minimum lot width, frontage, depth, and coverage; dwelling units per acre; parking spaces required; and maximum allowable height.

The purpose of zoning codes in Japan is similar to that of zoning codes in the United States: to maintain a favorable urban environment by controlling building use and ensuring the orderly arrangement of groups of buildings. Both the Building Standards Law and the City Planning Law cover zoning. The City Planning Law defines each zoning classification, and the Building Standards Law dictates what is allowed to be built in each category. Zoning restrictions are generally applicable only to City Planning Areas designated under the City Planning Law. City Planning Areas are divided into Urbanization Promotion Areas, where development can occur, and Urbanization Control Areas, where development is restricted.

Land use zones in Japan are classified into 12 general categories: low-rise residential districts 1 and 2; medium- and high-rise residential districts 1 and 2; residential districts 1 and 2; quasi-residential districts; neighborhood commercial districts; commercial districts; quasi-industrial districts; industrial districts; and exclusive industrial districts.

A Japanese zoning designation does not indicate, in and of itself, what can or cannot be built within that zone. For example, hotels and office buildings that meet the requirements of the Building Standards Law can be built in a residential district 2, a quasi-residential district, a neighborhood commercial district, a commercial district, or a quasi-industrial district. Hospitals, universities, and trade schools can be built in any district except a low-rise residential district 1 or 2, an industrial district, or an exclusive industrial district. Houses, condominiums, and apartments can be built in all districts except exclusive industrial districts. (Figure 4-1 provides more detailed information on zoning categories.)

FIGURE 4-1

Zoning Designations and Purposes

Zoning Designation	Purpose
Low-rise residential 1	Preserve a good atmosphere for low-rise residential buildings
Low-rise residential 2	Preserve a good atmosphere primarily for low-rise residential buildings
Medium- and high-rise residential 1	Preserve a good atmosphere for medium- and high-rise residential buildings
Medium- and high-rise residential 2	Preserve a good atmosphere primarily for medium- and high-rise residential buildings
Residential 1	Preserve residential atmosphere; large-scale stores or offices (larger than 3,000 square meters—32,290 square feet) prohibited
Residential 2	Preserve atmosphere primarily for residential buildings; large-scale stores and offices allowed
Quasi-residential	Preserve atmosphere for residential buildings in road-side areas; promote suitable businesses in such areas
Neighborhood commercial	Promote development of commercial and other businesses that mainly supply commodities for neighborhood
Commercial	Promote the convenience of commercial facilities; designated for commercial and other businesses
Quasi-industrial	Promote the development of industry that poses no risk to the environment
Industrial	Promote the development of industry
Exclusive industrial	Promote the development of industry exclusively

FIGURE 4-2

Maximum Floor/Area Ratios and Building-Coverage Ratios

Zoning Designation	Maximum Floor/Area Ratio (%)	Maximum Building-Coverage Ratio (%)
Low-rise residential 1	50 60 80 100 150 200	30 40 50 60
Low-rise residential 2	50 60 80 100 150 200	30 40 50 60
Medium- and high-rise residential 1	100 150 200 300	30 40 50 60
Medium- and high-rise residential 2	100 150 200 300	30 40 50 60
Residential 1	200 300 400	60
Residential 2	200 300 400	60
Quasi-residential	200 300 400	60
Neighborhood commercial	200 300 400	80
Commercial	200 300 400 500 600 700 800 900 1,000	80
Quasi-industrial	200 300 400	60
Industrial	200 300 400	60
Exclusive industrial	200 300 400	30 40 50 60
No zoning designation	100 200 300 400	50 60 70

Note: *The maximum floor/area and building-coverage ratios permitted in different zoning designations are decided by local government authorities. In principle, the local authorities choose one of the floor/area or building-coverage ratios shown in the table, depending on the zoning designation.*

Land use regulations are designed to prevent the undesirable mixing of uses and to protect living environments. The construction of certain buildings is therefore restricted under land use designations. Figure 4-2 lists the maximum floor/area ratios and the maximum building-coverage ratio for each zoning designation.

Additional regulations applicable to low-rise residential districts 1 and 2 include a height limit of ten or 12 meters (33 or 39 feet).

The slant line restriction and the sun-shadow restriction are unique to Japan. There are three types of slant line restriction: road slant line, adjacent building slant line, and north side slant line, all of which are designed to ensure ample space for natural light and ventilation between buildings. The permissible degree of slant is usually 1.25 for residential districts and 1.5 for

FIGURE 4-3

Zoning Designations and Road Slant Line Restrictions

	Zoning Category and Designation	Floor/Area Ratio (FAR)	Distance from Road Regulation[a] (Meters/Feet)	Slant Coefficient[b]
1	Low-rise residential 1 and 2	Less than or equal to 200%	20/66	1.25
	Medium- and high-rise residential 1 and 2	More than 200% and less than or equal to 300%	25/82	
	Residential 1 and 2	More than 300%	30/98	
	Quasi-residential (except structures that are in category 4)			
2	Neighborhood commercial and commercial (except structures that are in category 4)	Less than or equal to 400%	20/66	1.5
		More than 400% and less than or equal to 600%	25/82	
		More than 600% and less than or equal to 800%	30/98	
		More than 800%	35/115	
3	Quasi-industrial, industrial, and exclusive industrial (except structures that are in category 4)	Less than or equal to 200%	20/66	1.5
		More than 200% and less than or equal to 300%	25/82	
		More than 300%	30/98	
4	High-rise promotion district and residential use with FAR greater than or equal to 66%	All FARs	35/115	1.5
5	No zoning designation	Less than or equal to 200%	20/66	1.5
		More than 200% and less than or equal to 300%	25/82	
		More than 300%	30/98	

Note: With knowledge of a site's zoning designation and permitted floor/area ratio, it is possible to determine both the "distance from the road regulation" and the slant coefficient. By multiplying the slant coefficient by the width of the road, it is possible to determine the angle of the slant line to which the building height must conform. The slant line is drawn from the boundary of the opposite side of the road. The slant restriction will not apply to any part of the building that is located beyond the "distance from the road regulation."

a. The "distance from the road regulation" is measured from the boundary of the opposite side of the road.
b. The slant coefficient is used to determine the slant line, which is drawn from the boundary of the opposite side of the road.

FIGURE 4-4 **Slant Line Restrictions**

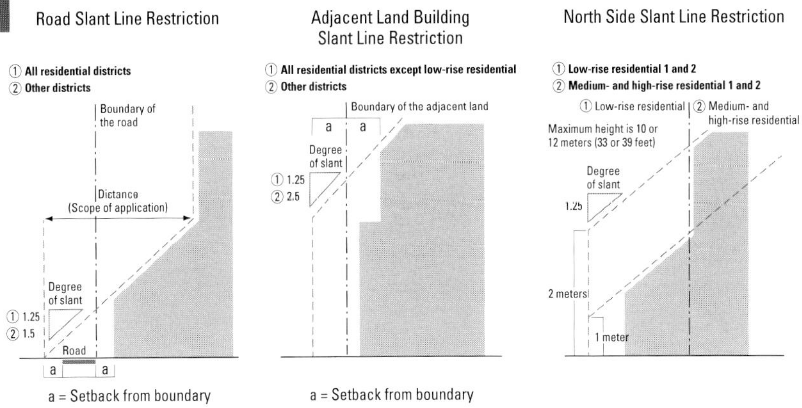

all other districts.[1] For a given building, the degree of slant is calculated according to the distance between the building and the boundary of the road that the building faces, or between the building and the boundary of an adjacent site. The calculation is also based on zoning designations and allowable maximum floor area. Figure 4-3 shows the permissible degree of slant for each type of zoning designation. Figure 4-4 provides graphic representations of slant line restrictions.

The sun-shadow restriction *(nichi ei kisei)* is a Japanese code that protects the rights of residents in congested city centers to receive ample sunshine in their homes. (Even Japanese families who live in plush condominiums prefer to air their bedding in sunlight and to hang their laundry outside to dry.) Sunshine rights *(nisshoken)* are legally codified in the Building Standards Law.

The sun-shadow restriction applies to low-rise residential districts 1 and 2; medium- and high-rise residential districts 1 and 2; residential districts 1 and 2; quasi-residential districts; neighborhood commercial districts; quasi-industrial districts; and areas that have no zoning designations. However, the restriction does not apply to commercial districts, industrial districts, or exclusive industrial districts. Thus, the developer of a high-rise condominium complex, for example, must conform to the sun-shadow restriction. Figure 4-5 shows building regulations based on the sun-shadow restriction.

FIGURE 4-5

Sun-Shadow Restrictions

Zoning Designation	Characteristics of Building Subject to Restrictions	Height at Which the Sun-Shadow Restriction is Measured[a]	Type of Shadow Restriction Assigned by Local Government[b]
Low-rise residential 1 Low-rise residential 2	With eaves over 7 meters (23 feet) high or with at least three stories, excluding basement	1.5 meters (five feet)	1 2 3
Medium- and high-rise residential 1 Medium- and high-rise residential 2	Over 10 meters (33 feet) high	4 meters (13 feet)	1 2 3
Residential 1 Residential 2 Quasi-residential Neighborhood commercial	Over 10 meters (33 feet) high	4 meters (13 feet)	1 2
Commercial	N.A.[c]		
Quasi-industrial	Over 10 meters (33 feet) high	4 meters (13 feet)	1 2
Industrial	N.A.		
Exclusive industrial	N.A.		
Nondesignated districts within City Planning Areas	Over 10 meters (33 feet) high	4 meters (13 feet)	1

a. Height refers in this case to the distance from the ground at which the sun-shadow restriction is measured. The greater the height at which the measurement is taken, the smaller the shadow length.

b. The local government decides which type of shadow restriction (shown in the two columns to the right) will apply in a particular case.

c. Not applicable.

Number of Hours of Shadow Time Permitted	
More than five meters (16.5 feet) and less than or equal to 10 meters (33 feet) from boundary	More than 10 meters (33 feet) from boundary
3 4 5	2 2.5 3
3 4 5	2 2.5 3
4 5	2.5 3
4 5	2.5 3
4	2.5

The Large-Scale Retail Store Location Law

The Ministry of Economy, Trade, and Industry is in charge of enforcing the Large-Scale Retail Store Location Law (Daiten Ritchi Ho), which applies to a retail store with a total sales area of over 1,000 square meters (10,765 square feet). The purpose of this law is to protect the living environment of nearby residents by regulating traffic, parking, bicycle stands, noise pollution, and waste management. The law also gives area residents an opportunity to voice their opinions on proposals to develop large-scale retail stores in their neighborhood. Both prefectural and city, town, or village agencies must evaluate and approve any applications to develop new, large-scale retail stores within their jurisdiction. This is one of the many bureaucratic hurdles that foreign investors must cope with when investing in Japan.

The permit process usually takes eight months, and should not take more than one year. The first two months are reserved to allow time for the retailer to hold neighborhood meetings to explain the store development plans. During the next two months, the local government (village, town, city) in which the proposed store will be located provides its opinion, along with residents, businesses, and any other interested parties. Four months are then set aside for the respective government agencies to make their final decisions. To comply with the required procedures, the retailer must receive feedback from the local government within eight months of completing the application. Revisions based on

Application Procedure for a Large-Scale Retail Store

Step 1: The retailer submits an application to construct a new large-scale retail store or add to an existing one.

Step 2: Over the next two to four months, the retailer

- Holds an informal meeting to make the application a matter of public record;
- Listens carefully to local opinions;
- Allows local residents, businesspeople, chambers of commerce, and local authorities to submit suggestions in writing.

Step 3: Over the next four months, the retailer obtains additional input from local governments. If there is no input, the procedure ends.

Step 4: Over the next two months, the retailer presents voluntary countermeasures to address any problems identified through public input.

If the voluntary countermeasures sufficiently protect the living environment, the procedure ends. If the input from the local government is not properly reflected and there is still concern about a negative influence on the living environment, the retailer will propose additional countermeasures. During this period, local municipal input continues, and final recommendations are obtained from the local government.

that feedback must be returned within two months after that. The large-scale retail store may not begin business operations until the review procedure is completed (see feature box).

Government Measures to Encourage Redevelopment

The Japanese government has enacted various schemes to facilitate redevelopment. For example, the Redevelopment District Plan (Saikaihatsu Chikukeikaku) was created to promote the redevelopment of large, underutilized areas. To encourage private sector involvement, certain designated areas offer special policies related to development. Local governments in these areas have the authority to relax some of the building codes, such as those that pertain to slant line restrictions and floor/area ratios. This scheme is currently being used in major metropolitan areas, including Tokyo's Shiodome district.

Another plan, the Urban Redevelopment Project (Shigaiichi Saikaihatsu Jigyō), promotes the redevelopment of underutilized land in downtown areas where there are many small plots of land owned by multiple parties. In addition to offering tax incentives and subsidies to developers, the Shigaiichi Saikaihatsu Jigyō helps developers find ways to amalgamate plots under multiple ownership. For example, the 11-hectare (27-acre), multibillion-dollar Roppongi Hills

A bottom-up view of some of the new high-rise buildings in the Shiodome redevelopment project.

project, completed in April 2003, was undertaken through the assistance of the Shigaiichi Saikaihatsu Jigyō.

The Urban Redevelopment Law (Toshi Saisei Ho), enacted in June 2002, is also designed to promote development. Under this law, developers who choose to invest in specially designated areas receive financial support from the Japanese government and may receive assistance to help shorten the development term. In some cases, building codes and zoning ordinances have been relaxed as well.

Structural Safety Measures

The first Japanese building code was introduced in 1924, in the aftermath of the 1923 Great Kanto Earthquake. Subsequent major earthquakes—mainly those in Hanshin Awaji (1955), Niigata (1964), Tokachi Oki (1968), and Miyagi Oki (1978)—have forced the Ministry of Land, Infrastructure, and Transport (MLIT) to continue to revise seismic provisions for buildings. The current laws and restrictions concerning design methods for buildings are specified in the Standards for Seismic Engineering Construction of 1980 and in the Order for Enforcement of the Building Law of 1981. The Order for Enforcement changed building design criteria associated with the magnitude and vertical distribution of earthquake motion and required the development of additional safety measures in case of a very large earthquake.

Japanese architects and engineers constantly apply knowledge gained from previous earthquakes to the construction and design of new buildings. It is safe to assume that buildings constructed since 1981 in accordance with the aforementioned

FIGURE 4-6

Probable Maximum Loss and Earthquake Risk

Probable Maximum Loss (%)	Degree of Risk	Expected Damage to Structure
0–10	Very low	Slight damage
10–20	Low	Partial damage
20–30	Medium	High possibility of moderate collapse
30–60	High	High possibility of major collapse
60 and over	Very high	High possibility of total collapse

laws—and in accordance with new requirements that have not yet been codified—are of higher quality than most buildings constructed prior to 1981.

There are three common types of construction: reinforced concrete structure, steel-reinforced concrete structure, and steel structure. The three types of frame are rigid frame, right frame plus load-bearing wall, and brace frame. The two types of foundation are spread foundation and pile foundation (which may be either prefabricated concrete pile, reinforced concrete pile, or steel pipe pile).

The seismic resistance of a building is evaluated in terms of the Structural Seismic Resistance Index (Is). This index shows the degree to which structural components, such as pillars and walls, are in balance in the building plan, the building's rigidity-weight ratio, and other factors that will affect seismic resistance.

The assessment of earthquake risk begins with an analysis of the area in which the building is located; on the basis of that analysis, an evaluation is undertaken that takes into account (1) data for past earthquakes and (2) any active faults that may affect the building site.

The most important index for assessing a building site is the probable maximum loss (PML). The PML is the maximum amount of damage that a building is likely to sustain as a result of a major earthquake with a 10 percent probability of occurring during a 50-year period. It is expressed as a percentage of the cost of totally reconstructing the building. For example, if a building with a real estate value of ¥20 billion ($184.6 million) is calculated to have a PML of 20 percent, then the building is projected to sustain ¥4 billion ($36.9 million) in damage during a major earthquake that has a 10 percent probability of occurring within 50 years. The lower the PML, the greater the value of the property for investment. If the PML of a building being considered for securitization exceeds 20 percent, the building will be assigned a lower rating for securitization.

Although the PML is often an important factor in deciding whether to purchase a building, it is important to be aware that the PML for a given building does not include damage to equipment, furniture, or stock; additional damage from flood or fire; compensation for victims; or losses from business interruption. Figure 4-6 shows the relationship between PML and earthquake risk.

As noted earlier, the Order for Enforcement of the Building Law of 1981 added strict new standards for building safety requirements. Reviews that have been undertaken of past projects indicated that buildings constructed after this law was enacted have PML ratios of less than 20 percent; the ratios of those constructed before the law average close to 30 percent. It is important for foreign investors to assess the degree of seismic hazards for a target property. The PML for an existing building is calculated on the basis of drawings and specifications. A calculation of PML can be requested when due diligence is performed.

The planning bureaus of some major metropolitan governments in Japan publish maps that use different colors to indicate the degree of potential earthquake danger. For example, the map of the Greater Tokyo Metropolitan Area depicts the level of risk associated with four types of dangerous conditions associated with earthquakes: danger from buildings, danger from fires, risk of human casualties, and risk of evacuation difficulties. The ratings are very high (5), high (4), medium-to-high (3), average (2), and low (1). A rating of 5 means that the area has poor soil, tightly packed wooden buildings, and many restaurants or factories that represent possible fire hazards. (See figure 4-7.)

Fire-Safety Standards

Japanese law designates two types of fire districts, to which different fire safety standards are applied: fire-prevention districts and quasi-fire-prevention districts. Fire-prevention districts are urban areas with a high density of commercial buildings, public buildings, industrial buildings, and mid- and high-rise residences. Quasi-fire-prevention districts are urban or nonurban areas with a moderate density of concrete and wooden buildings. If a development is located in an area that is designated as either as a fire-prevention district or a quasi-fire-prevention district, restrictions on building construction related to fire safety are applicable, based on the building's floor area or number of floors.

FIGURE 4-7

Index of Susceptibility to Collapse, Greater Tokyo Metropolitan Area

A building's susceptibility to collapse as the result of an earthquake depends mainly on the constitution of the soil on which the building stands and the structure of the building itself. Using data collected from the Great Hanshin earthquake, the Tokyo Metropolitan Government researched many buildings to determine their susceptibility to earthquakes. Criteria such as the structure, age, and height of the buildings were taken into account. Areas classified as particularly hazardous tend to have an abundance of aging buildings, constructed mainly from wood and lightweight steel, and to be located either in the center point of a naturally occurring basin or in alluvial land.

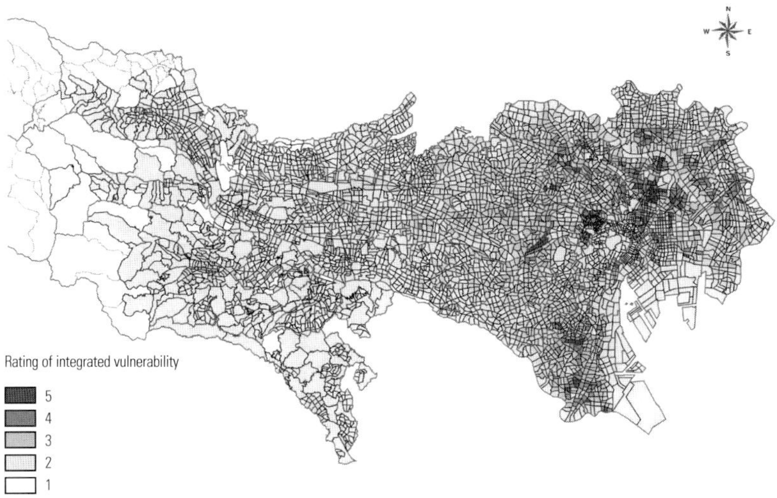

Map source: Fifth Earthquake Vulnerability Level Survey Results (2002), Bureau of City Planning, Tokyo Metropolitan Government.

Other restrictions on the kinds of building materials used and the types of buildings are as follows:

■ The principal building parts of a large-scale building (except floors, roof, and stairs) must be made fire resistant if the materials used are combustible, if the building is more than 13 meters (43 feet) high, has eaves more than nine meters (30 feet) from ground level, or has a floor area of more than 3,000 square meters (32,290 square feet).

■ Special buildings used by many people—such as theaters, auditoriums, concert halls, department stores, hospitals, hotels, and apartments—must be constructed of fireproof or quasi-fireproof building materials, as defined by Japanese law.

■ Fireproof buildings are those that are constructed from reinforced concrete and steel and that have approved fire-prevention coverings. They must have excellent structural stability during a fire and must be highly rated for their ability to prevent fire from spreading outside the building. Principal building parts (such as walls, posts, floors, beams, roofs, and stairways) must be of fireproof construction, and fire doors must be installed where necessary.

■ Quasi-fireproof buildings are those whose principal parts have either quasi-fireproof or a combination of quasi-fireproof and fireproof structure, or that have fire doors and fireproof external walls and are made of noncombustible building materials.

Fire-prevention codes require a certain amount of space between buildings and the use of fireproof external walls, partition walls, and fire doors. Restrictions on finishing materials are another means of preventing fire in buildings. The materials used for walls and ceilings must be made of noncombustible, quasi-noncombustible, or flame-retardant materials certified by the MLIT. The purpose of using such materials is to retard the initial outburst of fire and to control the amount of harmful smoke or gases released, thus helping to ensure safe evacuation. Noncombustible materials are concrete, mortar, brick, tile, asbestos panels, steel, aluminum, and glass. Flame-retardant materials are those that burn only slightly, without generating much smoke or gas, and that do not undergo harmful cracking, melting, or deformation.

Large-scale buildings, special buildings, or buildings with six or more floors must, in principle, have two or more stairways. In buildings where the stairway leads to a fifth floor (or higher) or to a second basement floor (or lower), the stairway needs to be designated an evacuation stairway, whose specifications are determined by law. Smoke exhausts must be installed to effectively reduce harmful smoke and gases from burning combustible building materials. Emergency lighting must also be provided for easy evacuation in case of power failure. Emergency doors must be installed in buildings that are more than three stories or that are 31 meters (102 feet) high or more, and emergency elevators must be installed for the use of firefighters. Furthermore, a passageway within the building must exit to an open space, such as a roadway, park, or public square; for large-scale wooden buildings, the passageway must be at least three meters (ten feet) wide; for all other buildings, it must be at least 1.5 meters (five feet) wide.

Note

1. *Degree of slant* refers to an imaginary line drawn from the top of a building to a point outside the building.

Chapter 5

Leasing Practices

It is important for foreign investors and tenants to be familiar with Japanese leasing practices, which differ significantly from those of Western countries. Of the various factors that contribute to these differences, one is the historic shortage of land suitable for commercial or residential buildings; because of this shortage, rental properties in prime locations and desirable vacant land parcels are both in short supply. The fact that many of the most prized trophy properties are owned by huge Japanese business conglomerates intensifies the problem. Thus, despite a prolonged recession, rental fees remain high, and lease conditions continue to be harsh. Another reason that rental fees remain high is the lack of downward market pressure: although the pattern is gradually changing, banks continue to provide financial assistance to companies saddled with huge debts; with little risk of foreclosure, companies have little incentive to fill vacant office space at lower rental rates.[1]

Japanese laws that pertain to leases are based on traditional Japanese business customs and practices, and may be confusing to Westerners. For example, a typical Japanese lease contract is much shorter and less detailed than a Western lease contract. And, although some companies that specialize in leasing to foreign tenants may use a Western-style rental contract, the terms and conditions of such contracts are not identical to those in Western contracts.

Land Leases

A land lease *(shakuchiken)* is the right to borrow land from a second party and use that land; this type of lease is used when a party owns a building but not the land on which it is situated. *Shakuchiken* has historically had two subcategories: (1) exclusive land lease *(chijoken)* and (2) leasehold *(chinshakuken)*. However, since it often gives an unfair advantage to the lessee, *chijoken* is very rarely used. Therefore, *chinshakuken* is the most common type of *shakuchiken*. In fact, in most cases the term *shakuchiken* is used to mean *chinshakuken*.

Chinshakuken refers to contractual rights obtained from a lessor-owner through a leasehold contract. Based on these rights, a lessee can demand continued assistance from the lessor to carry out the terms of the contract, even after taking occupancy of the land. For example, if a stone wall on the land collapses, the lessor remains obligated to repair the wall at his expense. At the same time, the lessee is not allowed to sublease the land without the consent of the lessor; nor can the lessee compel the lessor to have the leasehold contract registered. Unlike *chijoken* (exclusive land lease), *chinshakuken* (leasehold) does not hold the lessor responsible for registration of the contract; nor can the lessee petition the Land Court for such registration.

There are two main categories of *shakuchiken:* the "ordinary land lease"*(futsu shakuchiken)* and the "fixed-period land lease" *(teiki shakuchiken)*.

Ordinary Land Lease

The ordinary land lease *(futsu shakuchiken)* is the most widely used in Japan. The specific conditions of an ordinary land lease are as follows:

■ The length of the lease must be at least 30 years, but the parties to the contract can agree to make it longer. The length is calculated from the day after the signing (for example, a 30-year lease signed on October 23, 2000, will go into effect on October 24, 2000, and end on October 23, 2030). If the expiration date falls on a Sunday or a holiday, the lease can be extended until the following working day. If the building is destroyed during the initial period of the lease, the lessee is allowed, with the prior approval of the lessor, to tear it down and build a replacement structure. The lease for the new building period will be 20 years from either the date of approval or the date of completion of the construction, whichever is earlier, regardless of the length of the remaining lease period. However, if the lessor does not consent to the rebuilding, the lease period remains the same as under the original lease. Approval is assumed if the lessor fails to notify the lessee of an objection within two months of the lessee's request to rebuild.

■ The expiration of the lease term normally ends the lease, but the contract is automatically renewed if the building still exists at the time of expiration. The land lease will *not* be renewed, however, in either of the following circumstances: (1) both the lessor and lessee agree to allow the lease to expire and not to renew it (nonrenewal by mutual agreement), or (2) the lessor informs the lessee, without delay, of legitimate reasons for refusal to renew. A lessor who refuses to renew must prove that he has a need to use the premises that is stronger than the lessee's need to resume tenancy. (This is usually difficult for the lessor to prove.)

■ The first renewal period is 20 years and the second is ten.

■ The destruction and replacement of a building during a renewal period require the lessor's approval. If the lessee fails to obtain such approval, the lessor has the right to cancel the contract.

■ The terms of the lease can be revised by a petition from the lessee to the Land Court if the following conditions apply: (1) new ordinances or changes in surrounding land use conditions force a change in the current use of the land; or (2) the lease contract contains restrictions that prevent reasonable extension or rebuilding suitable to normal use of the land.

Fixed-Period Land Lease

The fixed-period land lease *(teiki shakuchiken)*, a new lease form based on a modified version of Hawaiian lease law and adopted by the Ministry of Land, Infrastructure, and Transport, was created to promote the more effective use of vacant land in residential areas. The rights of lessees have traditionally been very strong in Japan: even if the lease contract specifies a date of termination, lessees can hold onto leased land almost forever. As a result, landowners have always been reluctant to lease their land. Contracts under the Fixed-Period Land Lease System, which was implemented in 1992, alleviate landowners' concerns that a lessee may exercise his right to overstay the lease. Under such contracts, the lessee must vacate at the end of the contract term.

There are three forms of contract under this law: the "common fixed-period land lease" *(ippan teiki shakuchiken)*, the "land lease with special building-transfer conditions" *(tatemono joto tokuyakutsuki shakuchiken)*, and the "land lease for business purposes" *(jigyoyo shakuchiken)*.

Common Fixed-Period Land Lease. The conditions of the common fixed-period land lease *(ippan teiki shakuchiken)* are as follows:

■ The term of the lease is 50 years or more with no right of renewal beyond the stated period of time.

■ The lease expires automatically even if the lessee has legitimate reasons for renewal of the contract.

■ The expiration provision becomes effective even if the building still exists at the time of expiration.

■ The lessee, at his own expense, must remove all improvements on the premises and return the land to the lessor unless there is a special provision stating otherwise.

■ A lessee who claims that he did not remember the expiration date can petition the Land Court to protect his interests by extending the lease by no more than one year from the date on which the lessee remembered the expiration.

■ In many instances, the lessee is obligated to provide the lessor with a deposit, equivalent to as much as 20 percent of the land value, which will be kept by the lessor during the entire 50 years of the lease contract. The lessor is not obligated to pay any interest to the lessee and may commingle these funds with other funds.

While this land lease gives the lessor a guarantee of being able to recover his land at the end of 50 years, it has not been well received because the lessee must put up a large sum of money as a deposit at the very beginning of the lease contract.

Land Lease with Special Building-Transfer Conditions. A land lease with special building-transfer conditions *(tatemono joto tokuyakutsuki shakuchiken)* includes a special condition under which the lessee will sell the building to the lessor at a reasonable price after at least 30 years have elapsed. This form of land lease enables the lessor to cancel the lease contract, without any specified reason for cancellation, simply by buying the building. If the former lessee wishes to rent the building after the purchase, a lease contract can be executed for the building. (Such an arrangement is called a sale-and-leaseback in the United States.)

Land Lease for Business Purposes. The land lease for business purposes *(jigyoyo shakuchiken)* is designed specifically for commercial buildings and cannot be used for residential buildings or for office condominium buildings. A land lease for business purposes must be for a minimum of ten years and for a maximum of 20 years. Many of the restrictive conditions in ordinary land leases, such as those concerning length, renewal, rebuilding, and building transfer, are not applicable to this form of lease, which automatically expires at the end of the contract period.

Leasehold for a Temporary Use

When land must be used temporarily (e.g., for the offices of a contractor working at a construction site), a special form of leasehold—*ichijishiyo mokuteki no chinshakuken*—is used. This land lease is short-term and does not carry the restrictions of long-term leases. In many instances, however, it includes protective covenants and stipulations relating to rent increases or decreases.

Master Leasing of Commercial Property

Master leasing of commercial property is a special scheme under which a developer interested in a large commercial property will provide the landowner with between 80 and 90 percent of the initial construction costs (*kensetsu kyoryoku kin*—"construction cooperation money") and a deposit of between 10 and 20 percent. For example, if a landowner of a large parcel of land, suitable for a large-scale shopping center, wishes to develop the land but does not want to invest his own money, he can agree to give an anchor tenant the master lease for the shopping center. In exchange for a 20-year master lease, the tenant would pay the entire construction costs in advance. The landowner would then work with the anchor tenant to develop the shopping center in accordance with the tenant's specifications. The tenant can sublease portions of the shopping center to other tenants at high rents. After ten years, the tenant will receive a refund of the entire initial investment through ten annual installments. Although master-lease arrangements were common in the past for shopping center developments, they are beginning to be replaced by other types of land leases.

Building Leases

In comparison to the detailed and lengthy building leases used in Western countries, Japanese agreements are generally brief—perhaps only three to six pages. The main differences between Japanese and Western-style building leases concern the length of the lease terms; the payment of security deposits, key money, and rental agents' fees; termination procedures and tenants' rights; rent payment; rental-area measurement; maintenance and utilities payments; consumption (sales) and property taxes; depreciation fees; restoration of premises; and the need for joint surety or guarantors.

Lease Term

The typical Japanese office-building lease is for two years, with an implicit understanding that it will be automatically renewed. The lessee must notify the lessor of his intent to extend the lease six months prior to the expiration and must in many cases agree to pay a renewal fee equivalent to one month's rent.

The two-year lease term is used by the majority of Japanese lessors because the short-term lease protects them against the tenant's rights and allows them to routinely renegotiate the terms of the lease as market conditions change.

Security Deposit, Key Money, and Rental Agent Fee

It is customary in Japan for a tenant to pay a landlord a security deposit *(shikikin)* equivalent to six to 18 months' rent. (For a residential condominium or a single-family dwelling, the amount is usually two months' rent, but it is between 12 and 18 months' rent for office or retail space in a prime location.) This deposit is to ensure that the tenant will adhere to his obligations, as stipulated in the lease agreement. It is partially or fully refundable, depending on the condition of the leased premises when they are vacated. However, the landlord is not required to hold this deposit in escrow or to pay accrued interest to the tenant. Any interest earned is considered additional income for the landlord.

The tenant also customarily pays "key money" *(kenrikin)*, amounting to several months' rent, which is not refundable. (Key money in the case of residential leases is called *reikin,* rather than *kenrikin.*) This practice, however, has become less common in recent times. Key money is somewhat like the lease premiums paid in some Western countries to obtain very desirable property, but in Japan it is considered a gift to the landlord, as a token of the tenant's appreciation for being permitted to rent the property. Because of depressed market conditions in effect since the early 1990s, the amount of key money the tenant is expected to pay has decreased in some areas; in some instances, to entice a tenant to lease, the landlord may not even ask for any key money. Nevertheless, key money amounts remain high in other areas—particularly for prime retail locations in busy metropolitan shopping districts.

In the United States, it is the landlord who pays brokerage fees and advertising expenses, but in Japan the tenant pays a brokerage fee too, equivalent to one month's rent.

Termination Procedures and Tenants' Rights

Termination or eviction of a tenant is rather complicated in Japan because the landlord and tenant laws heavily favor tenants' rights. The landlord cannot simply expect the tenant to vacate the leased premises when the lease expires; the tenant is permitted to stay on unless the lessor can give the lessee legitimate reasons for the decision. A landlord who wishes to forcibly evict a tenant will have to convince the tenant to leave and be willing to pay "eviction compensation" *(tachinoki ryo)* even if the lease term has expired. This unique Japanese practice derives from the "lessee's right to continue occupancy" *(kyojuken),* which was originally meant to protect residential tenants from being thrown out by greedy landlords during the acute housing shortage after World War II. *Tachinoki ryo*—a certain percentage of the sales price, the value of the land lease to the tenant, and/or the anticipated profits from redevelopment—can be very substantial if the landlord expects to receive significant financial gains by terminating the lease. The landlord is also expected to pay the tenant's moving expenses—and even lost revenues, if the lease is for commercial space.

If a landlord refuses to renew a lease or increases the rent, a tenant can protest by petitioning the Land Court for arbitration. The tenant then sets up an escrow account *(kyotakukin koza)* with the court and pays the current monthly rent into the account while the appeal is pending. He must also notify the landlord of this action to avoid eviction for nonpayment of rent.

Rent Payment

Tenants of an office building or a multifamily residential building must pay rent for exclusively occupied space *(senyo menseki)* and a maintenance charge *(kanrihi* or *kyoekihi)*. Rent for a given month is paid either on the last day of that month or by the 25th day of the preceding month. Although in theory rents can be raised if drastic changes in economic circumstances occur, in practice rents are not increased until rental contracts become due for renewal.

For retail and restaurant spaces, percentage rent—a practice long used in Western countries, in which tenants pay a percentage of commercial income—is also popular in Japan.

Rental Area Measurement

The area of rental premises is measured from the center of each wall to the center of the opposite wall and is expressed in square meters, using the standards of the Building Owners and Managers Association International. However, the old *tsubo* measurement, which is based on the area of two tatami mats (a traditional Japanese floor covering found in houses, temples, and shrines), is still used even today. One *tsubo* is equal to 3.306 square meters (35.59 square feet); rent is calculated by multiplying the number of *tsubo* by the amount of rent per *tsubo*.

Maintenance and Utilities

The maintenance charge *(kanrihi* or *kyoekihi)* is a fixed fee paid by tenants for the upkeep of common areas and facilities, such as the entrance, lobbies, hallways, restrooms, elevators, air conditioning, and heating; and for the wages of security, maintenance, yard service, and cleaning staff. Since items covered by the maintenance charge differ from building to building, a tenant should confirm which items are included or excluded.

One aspect of the maintenance charge that may differ from Western practice is that the charge may be arbitrary and may not represent actual operating expenses. In some instances, an additional profit margin is built into the maintenance charge. The law does not require landlords to submit annual expense reports to tenants' associations, and tenants do not have the right to audit the landlord's expense records.

If the building has separate meters for utilities (water, electricity, gas), tenants pay the service providers directly. Tenants in older or smaller buildings that lack separate meters pay the landlord prorated utility charges based on the size of the space they occupy. Rent does not usually include parking, so each tenant pays a monthly parking fee to the landlord.

Consumption and Property Taxes

In addition to the monthly rent and maintenance charge, the tenant may be asked to pay a consumption (sales) tax of 5 percent to the landlord. The consumption tax is usually paid separately from rent to protect the landlord from double taxation. In some instances, however, the tax may be included in the rental amount. Regardless of which system is used, the landlord is required to remit 5 percent of the total for all rental receipts to the government.

In Japan, landlords pay three different property taxes: the fixed-asset tax *(koteishisan zei),* the urban planning tax *(toshikeikaku zei),* and the special landholding tax *(tokubetsu tochihoyu zei).* The fixed-asset tax applies to land, buildings, and depreciable assets used in business and is levied by the municipality in which these assets are located. The standard annual tax rate is 1.4 percent of the taxable value of the fixed assets. The urban planning tax, a surtax levied on top of the fixed-asset tax, applies to land and buildings in certain urban areas. The maximum rate allowed for this tax is 0.3 percent of the property value. The special landholding tax, which applies to those who either hold or purchase a parcel of land of more than a specified size, is 1.4 percent for landowners and 3 percent for buyers. Tax reforms passed in 2003 have temporarily suspended the special landholding tax.

In Japan, landlords' property tax obligations are not passed on to the tenant. This arrangement is quite different from the system of net leases found in many Western countries, under which landlords may pass on certain expenses, such as property taxes, to the tenant.

Depreciation Fee

The depreciation fee is a set percentage of the deposit money that the landlord retains upon expiration of the lease; it can be thought of as key money paid in arrears rather than in advance. In the case of smaller or privately owned buildings, the fee is equivalent to several months' rent. This system of collecting money from tenants illustrates the difference between Japanese and Western landlords in compensating for depreciation.

Restoration of Premises

In Japan, when a tenant vacates a leased property, it must be restored to its original condition. This occurs at the tenant's expense and includes repairs to all walls, floors, and ceilings, and the removal of any fixtures installed by the tenant. The restored condition is called "white box," which means that the property is totally empty and clean, without any fixtures. Landlords usually demand total restoration, and the costs can be very high.

Joint Surety and Guarantors

When a lessee enters into a contract in Japan, it is customary to have a company or individual guarantee the payment of rent and the lessee's proper conduct. This means that the signatory (lessee) and a guarantor *(rentai hoshonin)* are required to jointly complete a contractual agreement. Although the joint surety may not be necessary if the lessee is a Japanese branch office or subsidiary of a large, well-known multinational corporation, it is likely that the parent company will be asked to cosign the lease contract.

A foreigner who is leasing a property must find a guarantor who promises, by signing the contract, that he will be responsible for all financial matters and for anything that might go wrong during the contract period. The guarantor usually must be a Japanese citizen of good financial and moral standing. (A foreign resident holding a permanent resident visa is usually not qualified to be a guarantor.)

Building Limited-Term Lease

An ordinary building lease, like a land lease, favors the tenant: if the owner has no justifiable reason for terminating the contract, the tenant can renew after the expiration of the lease. The "building limited-term lease" *(teiki shakkaken)* introduced in March 2000, differs from an ordinary building lease in the following respects:

■ The lease contract will terminate, in accordance with the terms of the contract, with no right of renewal, if the owner provides notice at least six months before the expiration of the lease term.

■ The lease cannot be terminated prematurely except in certain specified cases.

■ Future rental fees may be determined as of the date of the contract through the execution of a special agreement.

The building limited-term lease is believed to have had a significant impact on Japan's real estate environment. The three principal effects are as follows:

- Because landlords need no longer wait for tenants to willingly vacate at the end of the lease, they can remodel and upgrade their facilities as necessary to stay competitive in the market.
- Under the old contract structure, landlords had legitimate fears that the tenant could force a lease extension, which made them reluctant to lease to tenants who were unfamiliar or difficult to investigate. The new contract structure has assuaged this fear, easing the rental market for foreign lease applicants and for those who are not familiar to the landlord.
- With a contract completion term upon which all parties can rely, the securitization of the property becomes feasible. Having a fixed date instills the necessary confidence in the lending banks that the building can be sold and the loan paid off. This greater level of certainty should accelerate the surge in property securitization and, consequently, the liquidity of the real estate market.

Office Leases

Office or retail agreements usually include specific provisions relating to permitted use, leased space, rights and obligations, fixture purchase (by the landlord), deposits, key money, and depreciation. An office or retail building may have many different tenants sharing the same premises, engaging in a variety of business activities, and receiving a large number of outside visitors. Typically, office buildings in Japan have retail shops and restaurants in the basement and lower floors. Any lease agreement, therefore, may have different terms and conditions depending on the type of the building, the landlord, the vacancy rate, the condition of the market, and other factors. In the case of an office building, the landlord usually completes the construction of the leased premises according to the lessee's specifications. However, in the case of a retail shop or restaurant building, the landlord commonly provides the "skeleton," but no construction or remodeling for the lessee.

The following terms and conditions are typically included in a lease for an office or retail space in Japan:

Article 1: Description of the premises. Specifies the name and location of the building and the type of structure, and gives the area of the premises in square meters. It is important to check the actual size of the premises against the blue-

Shinjuku was one of the first large-scale high-rise office developments in Japan. The area was developed in the 1970s, and is located west of Shinjuku Station, a major transportation hub that serves 3.25 million people each day.

print. The description of the premises must clearly indicate both exclusive and common areas; for contractual purposes, the combined area is the total space.

Article 2: Purpose of use. A specific description of the purpose, prohibited uses, and conditions for expansion or changes of use. The lessee must submit a construction plan in advance and obtain the lessor's consent to make changes to the interior, fixtures, or facilities. In many instances, the lessor may require the lessee to use a particular contractor and may refuse to allow an unknown lowest bidder to work on the construction project.

Article 3: Term of lease and renewal. The average lease term is between two and three years. Unless the lessor issues a notice of refusal at least six months before expiration, the initial term will automatically be renewed for another one or two years. The renewal fee is one month's rent at the new level.

Article 4: Rent, maintenance, and other charges. Monthly rent per *tsubo;* maintenance charge; electricity, gas, water, and telephone charges; and consumption tax. The rent and maintenance charge start when the lessee moves in; no grace period is given for construction or remodeling. The payments are made directly to the lessor's bank account by the last day of each month.

*Article 5: New rent.*The lessor has the right to revise the rent and maintenance charge in the event of unexpected economic changes (resulting, for example, from a tax increase or from increases in other charges). It is not uncommon for the lessor to raise the rent and maintenance charge at the time of renewal by giving written notice to the lessee. In some instances, the lessor may even ask the lessee to pay more rent during the term of an ongoing lease agreement.

Article 6: Security deposit. Today, the amount of security deposit is between six and 12 months' rent for office leases and between 12 and 18 months' rent for retail leases, depending on market demand. (During the bubble economy, landlords became accustomed to collecting unreasonably high deposits.)

Article 7: Refund of security deposit. The security deposit—minus any unpaid rent, maintenance charges, damages, depreciation fees, and other charges—is returned within six months of the end of the agreement. As it may be impossible for the lessee to return the premises in their original condition, as stipulated in the agreement, in almost all instances the lessee cannot expect a refund of the entire amount of the security deposit.

Article 8: Matters to be prohibited. Specifies prohibited actions, such as offering or assigning the lease right as a security without prior consent of the lessor; subleasing all or a part of the premises to a third party; permitting any other person to use the premises under any circumstances; claiming that third parties as residents; installing telephones, facsimile machines, Internet connections, or telex machines under the name of a third party; handling dangerous or combustible materials inside or outside the premises; and creating a nuisance for other tenants.

Article 9: Fixtures, refurbishing, and remodeling. Prior written consent is required for changes in, additions to, or removal of fixtures; for refurbishing or remodeling; for the installation of additional telephone lines, electrical equipment, or water pipes; and for any other such changes to the property. The lessor's prior consent must also be obtained when installing or posting a sign, notice board, or advertisement on the window glass, and when heavy objects (such as a metal safe) are moved into the building.

Article 10: Repairs to the leased premises. Repair and maintenance of the premises, as well as repairs to fixtures, interior, glass, fluorescent lights, and other appurtenances, are to be at the lessee's expense. The lessee must follow the lessor's instructions with respect to repairs and construction. The lessor bears the cost of repairing any damage to the main structure or to the main water pipes, gas pipes, and electrical wiring.

Article 11: Cancellation of the agreement by the lessor. If the lessee fails to pay the rental and maintenance charges for two months or more, the lessor is permitted, without prior notice, to immediately cancel the agreement. Cancellation is also allowed upon the commencement of legal actions such as attachment, provisional attachment, provisional disposition, auction, or any other public disposition or petition of bankruptcy against the lessee; upon notice of corporate reorganization, dissolution, or corporate rearrangement by the lessee; upon breaches or violations of the building regulations or public morals; or upon injury to the lessor's reputation by the lessee or his employees.

Article 12: Termination during the lease term. Either the lessor or the lessee may terminate the lease agreement before the term has expired by providing written notice at least six months before the expiration date. Instead of giving prior notice of termination, the lessee may terminate the agreement immediately by paying the lessor an amount equal to six months' rent.

Article 13: Entrance for inspection. The lessor or the lessor's representatives may, if necessary, inspect the premises with prior notice and the lessee's cooperation. In the case of an emergency such as fire or theft, however, no prior notice is necessary.

Article 14: Compensation for damages resulting from lessee's breach of agreement. The lessee will pay damages and standard costs at current prices.

Article 15: Compensation for damage to the premises. The lessee is required to pay the lessor compensation for any and all damage willfully or negligently caused by the lessee, his employees, contractors, or any other person.

Article 16: Damage claim by a third party. The lessee (1) accepts responsibility for any and all claims of damages by a third party, (2) will report on any settlement in court or out of court for such damages, and (3) will accept the waiver of the lessor's responsibility for claims by a third party.

Article 17: Lessor's immunity. The lessor will be given immunity from claims by the lessee for damages caused by natural disaster, calamities, theft, fire, and other causes not directly attributable to the lessor.

Article 18: Damage insurance. The lessor's casualty insurance will cover the premises during the term of the lease; the lessee is responsible for any insurance of the assets inside the building.

Article 19: Lessee's obligation of notification. The lessee is responsible for notifying the lessor in the event of (1) any change in the lessee's representative or trade name in Japan, (2) changes in the organization of the lessee's corporation in Japan, or (3) a change in the location of the lessee's head office in Japan.

Article 20: Termination of the agreement due to destruction. The lease will be terminated in the event of the destruction of, or significant loss of value to, the premises if such damage is caused by natural disasters, calamities, or any other occurrences not the fault of or attributable to the lessor or the lessor's actions; in such instances, no compensation will be given to the lessee except the return of the security deposit.

Article 21: Vacating the premises. The premises will be returned to the lessor in his presence in its original condition as described in the lease contract.

Article 22: Jurisdiction for contractual disputes. Specifies the jurisdiction in which disputes will be resolved.

Article 23: Joint surety. The lessee will provide a guarantee from a qualified individual or corporation approved by the lessor; if the original guarantor's financial soundness declines, the lessee will provide a suitable replacement.

Article 24: Special provisions. Consumption tax will be paid by the lessee.

Article 25: Notice, rules of use, and keys. Notice of any change of address of the lessee's head office will be posted within five days. The lessee must adhere to the rules of use specified in the contract The lessee will received two keys per door and will be responsible for the loss of the keys.

Article 26: Matters not provided for in the agreement. Doubtful points in the interpretation of any terms and conditions will be resolved through amicable settlement by mutual consultation between the both parties in good faith. (This is a unique provision included in almost all Japanese contracts.)

Residential Leases

Rental apartments and single-family houses are very scarce in Japan; consequently, rents are very high and lease conditions very strict. The lessor demands a large security deposit, a large amount of key money, a renewal fee, and a depreciation fee. A lessee usually needs to engage a rental agent to look for a suitable residence and must pay one month's rent for the service.

A Japanese residential lease agreement typically includes the following terms and conditions:

Article 1: Description of the premises. The name and address of the rental unit; a description of the type of structure (wooden, concrete, number of floors, etc.); a description of the space for the lessee's exclusive use; a list of facilities and appliances (water heater, washer and dryer, refrigerator, heating and cooling system, oven, microwave oven, telephone line, and parking spaces).

Article 2: Initial lease term. The lease term is two years, with an option for renewal.

Article 3: Rent. The lessee will pay rent monthly, directly into the bank account of the lessor, before the last day of the preceding month; rent for a period shorter than one month will be prorated on daily basis.

Article 4: Renewal of lease. Unless the lessee gives written notice of termination at least six months before the expiration date, the lease will automatically be renewed. It is customary for the lessee to pay one month's rent as a renewal fee.

Article 5: Utility charges. The lessee will be responsible for payment of all charges for electricity, gas, water, and telephone directly to the providers.

Article 6: Security deposit and key money. A security deposit of two months' rent and key money of two months' rent (not refundable) will be required. The deposit will be returned minus delayed rent, damages, and any other remaining financial obligations to the lessor, but no accrued interest will be paid. The lessee may not use the deposit as collateral.

Article 7: Cancellation by lessee. The lessee may cancel the lease by giving written notice at least two months before the expiration of the lease; less than two months' notice requires payment of a sum equal to the rent for the number of days by which the notice falls short of two months. The penalty for breaking the contract before the commencement of the lease is one month's rent. The penalty for cancellation within the first 12 months of the lease is also one month's rent.

Article 8: Cancellation by lessor. The lessor may cancel the lease under any of the following conditions: (1) with written notice at least six months before the expiration date, provided that there is a proper and justifiable reason; (2) with written 14-day notice for nonpayment of rent; (3) for detrimental acts committed on the premises that harm the reputation of the lessor; (4) for bankruptcy, incompetence, or death of the lessee (or reorganization, if the lessee is a corporation); or (5) for any violation of the building rules. It is important to understand that in Japan, a lessor cannot cancel a lease arbitrarily, without justifiable reasons—and, since it is very difficult to establish justifiable reasons, the lessor usually needs to negotiate with the lessee to arrive at a mutually acceptable amount of eviction compensation *(tachinoki ryo)*.

Article 9: Purpose of lease. The property will be for the exclusive use as a residence by the lessee and his family members.

Article 10: Prohibition of sublease. The premises cannot be subleased without the prior written consent of the lessor.

Article 11: Repairs. The lessee will notify the lessor of the need for repairs to any appliances, fixtures, or equipment included in the agreement; repairs or damage caused by negligence or mishandling will be at the lessee's expense; if responsibility for damage cannot be determined and the items in need of repair are not covered in the contract, responsibility for the cost of repairs will be decided by mutual agreement.

Article 12: Alteration. All repairs, renovation, and remodeling require the prior written consent of the lessor.

Article 13: Termination. Destruction or severe damage to the premises by fire, earthquake, or other causes beyond the control of either party will result in termination of the lease; in such an event, the lessor will not be held liable for any compensation except refund of the advance rent and security deposit.

Article 14: Entering the premises. The lessor or his employees may, with advance notice, enter the premises for inspection, repair, or cleaning; after notice of termination, the lessor or his employees may also, with proper advance notice, show the premises to prospective tenants.

Article 15: Vacating of the premises. The lessee agrees to move out immediately after expiration, cancellation, or termination of the lease, at his own expense; the lessee will be responsible for restoring the premises to their original state, apart from normal wear and tear.

Article 16: Taxes and insurance. Taxes and fire insurance premiums will be paid by the lessor, but the lessor will not provide insurance for the lessee's personal property.

Article 17: Report of change of guarantor. The lessee will notify the lessor immediately in writing of any change in the guarantor.

Article 18: Settlement of disputes. Any disputes will be settled according to the applicable landlord-tenant laws.

Article 19: Method of approval of changes. Any changes in the agreement will be in writing and by mutual consent of both parties or their lawful agents.

Article 20: Matters not provided for in the agreement. Resolution of any matters not addressed in the agreement will be accomplished through mutual consultation between the lessor and the lessee.

Article 21: Agreement on Japanese as official language. The Japanese-language version of the lease shall be accepted as the valid agreement; the English translation is provided for explanatory purposes only.

Note

1. A closely related factor is that lending institutions have, until very recently, been extremely slow to dispose of bad debt.

Chapter 6

Property Rights and Registration

In Japan, land parcels, buildings, and property rights are recorded in the registry book *(tokibo)* in the district where the real properties are located. The registration of real property ownership, leasehold rights, and mortgages is not absolutely mandatory under Japanese law; nevertheless, almost all these transactions, except leases, are registered in order to protect the interests of the parties involved.

In the United States, escrow companies take care of all the necessary documentation and safekeeping of funds associated with the transfer of property. In Japan, however, there are neither escrow companies nor title-guarantee companies. Consequently, buyers and sellers of real property must handle all the necessary processes personally, with the help of a judicial scrivener *(shihoshoshi)* or a Japanese lawyer *(bengoshi)*.

Osaka Business Park, located on a site formerly occupied by the Osaka Ordnance Works, is one of Osaka's primary skyscraper districts. Reclamation of the land was completed in 1984, and construction began shortly thereafter. The area covers 26 hectares (64 acres) and is located near Osaka Castle, a famous landmark.

Under current Japanese law, foreign lawyers are not allowed to engage in Japanese legal matters. They are classified as "foreign clerical lawyers" *(gaikokuho jimu bengoshi)* and are required to work with Japanese lawyers, even if the foreign lawyers speak Japanese and know Japanese law. American investors, who are accustomed to having their attorneys handle every phase of real estate transactions, may find it frustrating to personally engage in the registration of their real estate investments in Japan. Nevertheless, it is essential that they familiarize themselves with the unique Japanese system of registering real property, common methods of title search, proper procedures for the preparation of documents, methods of transferring funds, and other matters associated with real estate transactions.

Property Rights on Land and Buildings

In Japan, ten different kinds of real property rights can be registered: "exclusive and absolute right to real property" *(shoyuken)*; "right to superficies" *(chijoken)*; "easement right" *(chiekiken)*; "permanent tenancy right" *(eikosakuken)*; "preferential right" *(sakidori tokken)*; "pledge right" *(shichiken)*; "mortgage right" *(teitoken)*; "leasehold right" *(chinshakuken)*; "stone-quarrying right" *(saisekiken)*; and "redemption right" *(kaimodoshiken)*.[1] The registration of these various rights must be handled according to the Act Concerning Registration of Real Properties.

The registry book, which is housed in the registry office (also known as the legal affairs bureau) includes two sections: the Land Registry and the Building Registry. The "one real property for one form doctrine" *(ichi fudosan ichi toki yoshi shugi)* has been adopted for the registration of a land parcel or a building.

The registration form has three parts: a cover page *(hyodaibu)*, part A *(koku)*, and part B *(otsuku)*. The cover page includes a description of the property: for a parcel of

FIGURE 6-1

Example of Japanese Land Registry Document (Tokibo Tohon)

(Document available in Japanese only. English translation for reference only.)

Tokyo XX
東京都○○ Full Record with All Details
全部事項証明書 Land
（土地）

Cover Page 【表題部】	(Land Details)（土地の表示）		Record DateXXXX/XX/XX 調整: 平成○年○月○日	Map No. 地図番号	Blank 余白
Location 【所在】	Tokyo XX 東京都○○				
Plot No. 【①地番】	Type of Land Use 【②地目】	Area 【③地　積】　m2	Reason for Entry & Date 【④原因及びその日付】		Date of Registration 【登記の日付】
XX (Number) 番○○	Residential Site 宅地	No.XX 第○○	Blank 余白		Blank 余白
(Other Entries)					

Part A 【甲　区】	Matters Concerning Ownership Title（所有権に関する事項）			
Ranking 【順位番号】	Purpose of Registration 【登記の目的】	Date of Receipt, Receipt No 【受付年月日・受付番号.】	Reason 【原因】	Right Holder & Other Information 【権利者その他の事項 】
1	Transfer of ownership 所有権移転	XX/XX/XX (Date of Receipt) XXX (Receipt Number) 平成○年○月○ 第○○	Sold on XX/XX/XX (Date) 平成○年○月○日売買	Owner Tokyo XX (Owner Address) A Company (Owner Name) Recordation of Transfer of Title Rank 1 所有者　東京都○○ A 株式会社 順位1番の登記を移記
(Other Entries)				

Part B 【乙区】	Matters Concerning Rights BesidesOwnership Title（所有権以外の権利に関する事項）			
Ranking 【順位番号】	Purpose of Registration 【登記の目的】	Date of Receipt, Receipt No 【受付年月日・受付番号】	Reason 【原因】	Right Holder & Other Information 【権利者その他の事項 】
1	Establishment of Mortgage 抵当権設定	XX/XX/XX (Date of Receipt) XXX (Receipt Number) 平成○年○月○日 第○○	On XX/XX/XX (Date) Establishment of Loan Contract on Same Date 平成○年○月○日金銭消費貸借同日設定契約	Loan Amount XX Million Yen Interest XX% Annual Damage Interest XX% Annual Debtor Tokyo XX (Debtor Address) A Company (Debtor Name) Mortgagor TokyoXX (Mortgagor Address) B Company (Mortgagor Name) 債権額 金○○万円 利息　年○% 損害金　年○% A 会社 抵当権者　東京都○○ B 会社
(Other Entries)				

This document certifies all details recored in the "Tokibo".

XX/XX/XX (Date)
XXX (Issuing Legal Affairs Bureau)　XXX (Name of Register of Legal Affairs Bureau)

これは登記簿に記録されている事項の全部を証明した書面である

平成○年○月○日
東京都法務局　　　登記官　○○

land, the property's location, and a classification in terms of the type of land and the amount of acreage; for a building, the location, number, type of structure, and floor space. Part A lists the names of all current and previous owners; it also includes general information pertaining to the ownership of the property, such as records of past transactions, special buyback clauses, interim registrations, preliminary injunctions, and attachments and other encumbrances. Part B includes all other information regarding rights to the property (e.g., superficies, permanent tenancy rights, easements, preferential rights, pledges, mortgages, and leaseholds).

If one property has many owners, it must be registered under the name of the main representative and show his address. In the past, the names, addresses, and ownership shares of all co-owners had to be attached to the registration form. However, because of recent changes in registration procedures that have resulted from the use of computers, it is no longer necessary to make a separate list of co-owners: they are all on record. Similarly, it is no longer necessary to maintain a separate list of all creditors and mortgagors, because they will all be listed in the computer.

Types of Registration

There are two types of registration: final, or definitive, registration *(shyukyoku toki* or *hon toki)* and preliminary registration *(yobi toki)*. Final registration is similar to the registration of real property in the United States, which serves as constructive notice to the public. Preliminary registration is not legally binding and may or may not result in definitive registration. There are two types of preliminary registration: advance-notice, or warning, registration *(yokoku toki)*, and interim registration *(kari toki)*.

A clerk of the court executes advance-notice registration to inform third parties that a suit seeking elimination or reversion of the existing registration has been filed against the owner. Advance-notice registration carries no legal power to invalidate or protest the existing registration.

Interim registration is recorded when actual, factual, or formal requirements for final registration have not yet been met. If a party applies for an interim registration on real property, the date of the interim registration will become the effective date of the final registration if that party later decides to apply for final registration. It is because the date of the final registration will revert back to the date of the interim registration that another party must take care to ensure that no interim registration exists on the property. However, it should be noted that interim registration cannot prevent a property owner from selling a property to a third party or putting mortgage loans on it before the final registration is completed.

Interim registration on the transfer of ownership is allowed under the following conditions: (1) when a seller will not cooperate with the buyer to apply for final registration; (2) when, on the basis of a sales contract, the buyer holds the right to transfer the title of the property; (3) when a purchase contract becomes effective on a certain future date; (4) when the title document is missing or lost, so the title holder cannot submit it for final registration; or (5) when a required certificate of approval or consent from a third party is unavailable and cannot be attached. However, interim registration is not allowed when the parties to a transaction cannot produce a certificate of seal *(inkan shomei)*, appear in person, submit a certificate of residence *(kyojushomei)*, or produce a certificate of cause of registration. Interim registration is also prohibited when the parties to a transaction do not have the money for the registration fee. The certificate of seal is issued by a local government and is used for the registration of real property and other important business transactions. The certificate of residence is issued by the local government to those who live in the district.

Title Search

Since there are neither escrow companies nor title-insurance companies in Japan, it is extremely important to conduct a thorough title search on a real property and fully investigate all legal rights attached to it. All records of real estate transactions in the registry office are open to the public, and any interested party is allowed to view and obtain certified copies of those records by filling out an application and paying a fee.

There are two kinds of title documents in Japan: the full title document *(tokijiko zenbu shomeisho)* and the abstract of the title document *(tokijiko ichibu shomeisho)*.[2] The full title document is a copy of the registered document and includes all the entries in the official registry; the abstract of the title document includes only those parts of the record requested by the applicant or user. In any title search, it is prudent to request the full title document, have it translated into English by a professional translator, and review every recorded entry carefully.

For foreign investors who would be inclined to trust the validity of documents registered in the Japanese system, it may be disconcerting to know that in Japan, the doctrine of trust in public documents *(koshin no gensoku)* does not apply with regard to real estate transactions. However, a third party of good conscience is protected by the civil law from false representations, which provides a safety net similar to that provided by the doctrine of trust in public documents. Likewise, an "implied credibility of registration" *(toki no suiteiryoku)* is assumed, according to which information in title documents is in principle accurate, unless definitive proof of the opposite is available.

If registration was done fraudulently, however, with false documentation, it is difficult for the registrar to determine the validity of transfer. The registrar simply conducts registration of real estate transactions on the basis of the written documents that are submitted; he has no direct involvement in the transactions. Therefore, before closing, investors must study the registration records carefully—which may require reviewing ownership records dating back as far as 20 years—to ensure that there are no longer any encumbrances on the property.

Because certain property rights are difficult to search using only those documents recorded in the registry office, the following steps should be taken to avoid mistakes in title search:

■ Check to see whether any leases have been made. If a building is registered in a name other than that of the landowner, it can be assumed that a land lease exists. If this is the case, it is advisable to meet the building owner in person and determine what type of lease exists.

■ Determine whether a mortgage loan has been placed on the building. If such a loan exists, it may establish "exclusive land lease established by law" *(hotei chijoken)*. This form of lease can be established only when (1) both the land and the building belong to the same owner and (2) either the land or the building is to be transferred to another owner in payment of debts due to foreclosure. The registration on the building will show whether it has been registered in the same name as that of the landowner and whether a mortgage has been placed on it.

■ Check thoroughly for property rights that may not be registered. Although almost all real estate transactions are registered, registration may, in some situations, be intentionally delayed or simply not executed. For example, to save the time and cost of registration, new houses and buildings are often transferred to new owners prior to registration. The following property rights are not usually registered or cannot be registered: "right to use under the Condemnation Law" *(tochishuyohojo no shiyoken)*; "building lease under the Land and Building Lease Law" *(shakuchishakkahojo no tatemono chinshakuken)*; "land lease under the Agricultural Land Law" *(nochihojo no chinshakuken)*; and "disaster victims' priority building lease right" *(risai shakkanin no tatemono yusen chinsakuken)*.[3]

Application Documents for Registration

Documentation for the registration of real property and property rights varies according to (1) what types of registration are required and (2) what is to be registered. Common types of registration are "registration of changes" *(henko toki)*; "registration of corrections" *(kosei toki)*; "registration of elimination" *(massho toki)*; "registration of recovery" *(kaifuku toki)*; and "registration of additions" *(kiyu toki)*, which includes "registration of continued ownership" *(shoyuken hozon toki)*, "registration of mortgages" *(teito settei toki)*, and "registration of transfers" *(shoyuken iten toki)*.

For the first-time registration of a land parcel, it is necessary to provide the name and address of the landowner, the location and address of the land, classification, and acreage. For the first-time registration of a building, it is necessary to provide the name and address of the building owner; the location of the building; its type (office, residential, retail, etc.), structure (steel, wood, etc.), floor space, and building number; and the type, structure, and floor space of any annex.

According to the Law Concerning Registration of Real Estate, the building owner is required to apply for registration of the property within one month after completing a new building.[4] Failure to apply for registration may result in a fine of up to ¥100 million ($923,800). To qualify to apply for registration, an applicant must submit a receipt of property tax payment. For a land parcel, attachments to the application must include the surveyor's map and land location map; for a building, attachments must include a drawing of the building and a floor plan for each floor of the building. In the case of an application for the registration of a new building, submission of the construction confirmation certificate *(kenchiku kakunin shosho)*, the inspection completion certificate *(kensa shomeisho)*, and the contractor's certificate *(ukeoinin no shomeisho)* is required.

The registration and license tax for registration of continued ownership is 0.2 percent (until March 31, 2006, and 0.4 percent thereafter) of the property value. The registration and license tax for registration of mortgage rights, preferential rights, or pledge rights is 0.4 percent of the amount of the obligation or loan value. The tax on the transfer of property is generally 1 percent (until March 31, 2006, and 2 percent thereafter) of the property value. (This tax rate does not apply to the transfer of property by inheritance.)

For registration of property rights, such as transfer of ownership or placement of mortgage, both the buyer or mortgagee *(toki kenrisha)* and the seller or mortgagor *(toki gimusha)*—or their attorneys-in-fact—must apply jointly.[5] The literal translation of *toki kenrisha* is "a person entitled to registration" or "a person who holds the right to demand registration"; this person, who may be either a buyer or a mortgagee, expects to receive benefits from the registration. The literal translation of *toki gimusha* is "a person who is obligated to register"; this person, who may be either a seller or a mortgagor, expects to lose the benefits of holding a real property or the associated rights.

In principle, applicants must come to the registration office in person.[6] In some cases, however, if all that is involved is simple confirmation of a transaction and entry into the registry, it is possible to register a transaction through an attorney or by mail.

To register a transfer of real property, an applicant must submit six important documents as attachments:

- A certificate of grounds for registration *(toki genin shomeisho)* or a copy of registration *(shinseisho fukuhon)*. When ownership is transferred through a sale, the certificate of grounds for registration is the sales contract for the transaction. Once either of these documents—the certificate of grounds for registration or the copy of registration—is duly registered, it becomes the certificate of title.
- The seller's registered certificate of title *(toki gimusha no toki-zumi shosho)* or the affidavit of witnesses *(hoshosho)*. If the seller's certificate of title is lost or destroyed, a duplicate cannot be reissued. In such a case, two people of legal age who have previous experience with registration procedures must sign an affidavit attesting that the seller is the same person who is to be registered as the owner of the property in question. The affidavit must be issued, along with the witnesses' certificate of seal, no more than three months before the application for registration. If the seller applies for registration with this affidavit, the registrar will contact the seller for clarification of all facts. If the seller does not reply in writing within three weeks of the notice, the application will be rejected.

FIGURE 6-2

Legal Affairs Bureaus and Regional Branches

District	Main Office	Regional Bureau	Jurisdiction
Tokyo	Tokyo Legal Affairs Bureau		Tokyo metropolitan area
		Yokohama	Kanagawa Prefecture
		Urawa	Saitama Prefecture
		Chiba	Chiba Prefecture
		Mito	Ibaraki Prefecture
		Utsunomiya	Tochigi Prefecture
		Maebashi	Gunma Prefecture
		Shizuoka	Shizuoka Prefecture
		Kofu	Yamanashi Prefecture
		Nagano	Nagano Prefecture
		Niigata	Niigata Prefecture
Osaka	Osaka Legal Affairs Bureau		Osaka area
		Kyoto	Kyoto area
		Kobe	Hyogo Prefecture
		Nara	Nara Prefecture
		Otsu	Shiga Prefecture
		Wakayama	Wakayama Prefecture
Nagoya	Nagoya Legal Affairs Bureau		Aichi Prefecture
		Tsu	Mie Prefecture
		Gifu	Gifu Prefecture
		Fukui	Fukui Prefecture
		Kanazawa	Ishikawa Prefecture
		Toyama	Toyama Prefecture

■ The certificate of legal representation *(dairi kengen shosho)*. The certificate of legal representation awards power of attorney to a third party, usually a judicial scrivener, to represent the applicant. If a company applies for registration through its representative director, it is permissible to use a certified copy of the company registration as the certificate of legal representation. The certified copy of the company registration can be either a full document or an abstract, but it must be issued by the registration office no more than three months prior to the date of application and must show the names of the officers who are authorized to sign the documents.

■ Permits, agreements, or consents by a third party *(daisansha kara no kyoka, toki, shodaku)*. If permits, agreements, or consents from a third party are

FIGURE 6-2

Legal Affairs Bureaus and Regional Branches (Continued)

Hiroshima	Hiroshima Legal Affairs Bureau		Hiroshima Prefecture
		Yamaguchi	Yamaguchi Prefecture
		Okayama	Okayama Prefecture
		Tottori	Tottori Prefecture
		Matsue	Shimane Prefecture
Fukuoka	Fukuoka Legal Affairs Bureau		Fukuoka Prefecture
		Saga	Saga Prefecture
		Nagasaki	Nagasaki Prefecture
		Oita	Oita Prefecture
		Kumamoto	Kumamoto Prefecture
		Kagoshima	Kagoshima Prefecture
		Miyazaki	Miyazaki Prefecture
		Naha	Okinawa Prefecture
Sendai	Sendai Legal Affairs Bureau		Miyagi Prefecture
		Fukushima	Fukushima Prefecture
		Yamagata	Yamagata Prefecture
		Morioka	Iwate Prefecture
		Akita	Akita Prefecture
		Aomori	Aomori Prefecture
Sapporo	Sapporo Legal Affairs Bureau		Hokkaido Prefecture
		Hakodate	Hokkaido Prefecture
		Asahikawa	Hokkaido Prefecture
		Kushiro	Hokkaido Prefecture
Takamatsu	Takamatsu Legal Affairs Bureau		Kagawa Prefecture
		Tokushima	Tokushima Prefecture
		Kochi	Kochi Prefecture
		Matsuyama	Ehime Prefecture

required, the applicant must obtain such documents from the third party and attach them when applying for registration. For example, the governor of the prefecture in which the land is located must approve the transfer of farmland with an area greater than four hectares (ten acres).

■ The seller's certificate of seal *(toki gimusha no inkan shomeisho).* If the applicant is an individual, the certificate of seal is certified by the mayor of the city, village, or town where the applicant resides. If the applicant is a corporation, the certificate of seal is certified by the registry office where the corporation is registered. If the seals of the officers of that corporation are registered in the same registry to which application is being made, it is not necessary to produce the certificate of seal.

■ The buyer's certificate of residence *(toki kenrisha no jusho shomei)*. Submission of the certificate of residence is required to ensure that the address of the buyer to be recorded in the registry is the same as that of the buyer's actual residence. If the applicant is an individual, the certificate of residence will be a copy of the certificate of residence *(juminhyo)*. If the applicant is a corporation, the certificate of residence will be a certified copy of the company registration.

There are 50 registry offices in eight separate districts: Fukuoka, Hiroshima, Osaka, Nagoya, Sapporo, Sendai, Takamatsu, and Tokyo. Figure 6-2 lists the locations of registry offices and branch offices.

Notes

1. Two other rights that are not recorded are "exclusive occupancy right" *(senyuken)* and "commonage right" *(iriaken)*.
2. *Tokibo tohon* was recently renamed *tokijiko zenbu shomeisho*; *toxibo shohon* was renamed *tokijiko ichibu shomeisho*. The older names, however, are still more commonly used by real estate industry professionals.
3. A thorough legal explanation of this last type of lease right is beyond of the scope of this book. For more detailed information, readers should refer to the Civil Code, Article 388, or consult their attorney.
4. Article 80, paragraph 3; Article 93, paragraph 3.
5. An attorney-in-fact is an individual who has power of attorney—that is, he has been given the power to act on behalf of the principal. An attorney-in-fact need not be a lawyer.
6. In accordance with Article 26, paragraph 1, of the Law Concerning Registration of Real Estate.

Chapter 7

Real Estate Investment Financing

Financing of real estate properties in Japan requires a good understanding of both traditional Japanese financing practices and new financing schemes that have been introduced recently. Because of the age-old Japanese belief that land has an intrinsic value—and that land prices would therefore never go down—Japanese commercial and trust banks have traditionally granted loans on real properties primarily on the basis of land value rather than improvements. And, as the focus was mainly on appreciation in land value, little attention was paid to cash flow or to return on investment.

Japanese lenders have always considered land the best collateral; and indeed, land values skyrocketed during the many decades before the collapse of the bubble economy, early in the 1990s. In addition to providing land as collateral, borrowers had to provide personal guarantees of repayment; and, until recently, there were no nonrecourse loans. Thus, parent companies were often required to cosign loan documents for their subsidiaries; presidents of corporations were routinely asked to put up personal assets as collateral; and individual borrowers were usually required to ask a relative or friend to cosign a mortgage loan.

Because project financing, as such, has not really existed in Japan, loans are not necessarily based on the merits of the project itself but on the borrower's creditworthiness.[1] During the past few years, however, in the face of stiff competition from foreign banks that are marketing nonrecourse loans and project financing, Japanese commercial banks and other financial organizations have begun to offer them as well.

Foreign investors have typically brought their own equity capital when investing in Japan. Recently, foreign investors have begun to obtain debt financing from Japanese commercial banks, from the Development Bank of Japan, or from foreign financial institutions operating in Japan. However, these financial institutions offer different types of loans on different terms and conditions than those commonly found in the foreign investors' country of origin. In addition, many investors prefer to take advantage of the Special-Purpose Company Law to execute financing arrangements, as it offers unique advantages for them. (Special-purpose companies will be discussed in a later section of this chapter.)

Nongovernmental Financial Institutions

There are a number of different kinds of regular banks *(futsu ginko)*, long-term finance institutions *(choki kinyu ginko)*, small- to medium-sized-enterprise finance institutions *(chushokigyo kinyukikan)*, and agriculture, forestry, and fishery finance institutions *(noringyogyo kinyukikan)*.

Regular banks are divided into city banks *(toshi ginko)*, regional banks *(chiho ginko)*, and secondary regional banks *(daini chiho ginko)*. These banks are licensed under the Banking Law to engage mainly in such financial activities as taking deposits, making short-term loans, and providing foreign exchange. The funds from deposits are lent to corporations for their operating expenses and equipment purchases, and given to individuals as mortgage loans.

City banks are large-scale banks with an extensive nationwide network of branches; their main offices are located in large cities. Major city banks, such as the Bank of Tokyo-Mitsubishi Ltd.; Mizuho Bank Ltd.; Resona Bank Ltd.; Sumitomo Mitsui Banking Company, Limited; and UFJ Bank, Limited, have large amounts of funds available for lending and engage in a variety of financial activities.

Regional banks are located in key regions and provide local financial services. Most of these banks are smaller than the city banks, but they have a good share of local banking business as they maintain close ties with local businesses and public institutions. Secondary regional banks are smaller than regional banks, and were formerly mutual banks for small- to medium-sized businesses. In response to the 1988 recommendation of the Finance System Research Council, they were converted into regular banks. (The preceding classifications, incidentally, are not based on the Banking Law but on custom and tradition.)

Long-term finance institutions are fewer in number than regular banks and are located in large metropolitan areas. They generate funds by issuing loan trusts and bonds, and they mainly provide long-term loans to larger corporations and public institutions.

Long-term finance institutions are classified into long-term credit banks and trust banks. Long-term credit banks operate in accordance with the Long-Term Credit Bank Law. Trust banks operate under the Banking Law but are allowed to engage in trust businesses. Because of the financial liberalization in 1985, foreign banks are now allowed to operate as trust banks. In 1993, stock brokerage companies and other finance companies were also permitted to enter into the trust business by establishing subsidiaries, which led to the creation of a number of additional trust banks.

Small- to medium-sized-enterprise finance institutions, as the name suggests, are finance companies that specialize in providing financial services to small and medium-sized enterprises. These institutions are private companies, but 70 percent of their funds are provided by the national government. In addition to collecting deposits, they are allowed to issue bonds to generate funds. Although their functions are limited, they can provide better loan terms and conditions than larger organizations can. These institutions include credit unions, credit associations, and commercial and industrial central credit associations.

Credit associations are larger than credit unions, and their scope is limited. Although nonmembers can make deposits, loans are given only to small or

Otemachi Marunouchi, Tokyo's financial district, is located next to Tokyo Station (Japan's central transportation hub), and is home to some of the world's largest banking and investment firms. Property prices in this area are the highest in the country.

medium-sized enterprises or to individuals that are members of the association. Credit unions are much smaller in scale, and only those individuals or small or medium-sized enterprises that are members of the credit union may maintain accounts or obtain loans.

The agriculture, forestry, and fishery finance institutions provide services for the primary industries of Japan, such as farmers' associations and fishery associations. Not only do they receive deposits and give loans to members, but they also provide marketing assistance for their members' products.

In addition to the financial institutions just discussed, other finance companies that have been providing real estate financing in Japan include life insurance companies; casualty insurance companies; nonbanking organizations, such as credit card companies and leasing companies; consumer finance companies; investment trust companies; stock brokerage companies; and short-term-loan companies. Three of the major life insurance companies are Daiichi Mutual Life Insurance, Nippon Life Insurance, and Sumitomo Life Insurance; there are about 40 other major life insurance companies.

Government-Sponsored Financial Institutions

There are some 14 government-sponsored financial institutions that play specific roles in servicing segments of key Japanese industries. However, only the Development Bank of Japan is commissioned to promote foreign direct investment in Japan. Wholly owned by the government and capitalized at ¥865.4 billion ($8 billion), the bank employs 1,387 staff members who provide a wide range of financial services to both domestic and foreign corporations.

The bank's stated mission is to promote economic revitalization and the creation of self-reliant regions, and to enhance the quality of life. Its major objectives are the following:

- To supply long-term, fixed-rate, low-interest loans, debt guarantees, and other types of assistance, in collaboration with private sector financial institutions;
- To provide project support by promoting smooth formulation of projects (from concept to planning and commercialization);
- To provide research reports on economic, social, industrial, and local trends.

The Development Bank of Japan gives support to Japanese companies that derive at least one-third of their capital from foreign sources, and to branches of foreign companies registered in Japan. The conditions of lending are as follows:

- Currency and jurisdiction: yen-based loan subject to Japanese lending laws;
- Interest rates: fixed at the time of disbursement;
- Maturity: average of 15 years, but up to 25 years;
- Grace period: up to three years;
- Repayment schedule: regular installments on principal;
- Collateral or guarantor: collateral or a guarantor (parent company) usually required;
- Application: one month usually required, but prior consultation may be necessary;
- Other conditions: no loan processing fees are charged, but stamp tax is required by law to be paid at the consummation of the loan agreement.

This loan program has a number of advantages:

- The loans have both long-term flexibility and fixed, low interest rates not available from commercial banks.
- The long grace periods may reduce the burden of capitalization at the initial stages of project development.

- The fixed interest rates, which may not be available with commercial bank loans, reduce the risk of interest-rate fluctuation.
- The bank finances only 40 or 50 percent of the project cost and allows co-financing with commercial banks.
- To supplement new investors' credit, the bank offers guarantees on commercial bank loans, at the guaranteed rate of 0.3 percent per annum of the outstanding balance.

In addition, the Development Bank of Japan does the following:

- Provides important information about the Japanese market, including reports on the current state of various industries (e.g., market scale and distribution networks);
- Provides capital consulting services and information about particular regions, to assist with decision making;
- Will help find suitable sites for investment;
- Provides assistance in conducting feasibility studies;
- Can draw on its large client base to introduce potential Japanese partners for joint ventures and sales connections.

Finally, the Development Bank of Japan also operates overseas, with representative offices in Los Angeles; New York; Washington, D.C.; Frankfurt; London; and Singapore.

The Development Bank of Japan reports that in 1998, the number of loans to foreign-affiliated companies reached 683, with a total loan value of ¥629 billion ($5.8 billion). Notable examples of companies receiving loans were Advanced Ceramics, AMP, Applied Materials, Boston Scientific Corporation, DuPont, Eli Lilly, General Electric, Interlink Electronics, International Rectifier, Lam Research, L.L. Bean, LSI Logic, MEMC Electronic Materials, Motorola, Nanometorics, Proctor & Gamble, Rohn and Hass, R.P. Scherer, Sequent Computer, Spraying System, Starbucks, Toys "R" Us, Tycon Corporation, Tylan General, and Watkins-Johnson.

Foreign Financial Institutions and Investment Companies

Japan's real estate market is the second-largest in the world, despite the fact that it has been extremely depressed for more than a decade and that continued declines in valuation are expected. In search of deals on distressed properties, major foreign financial institutions and real estate investment companies have poured billions of dollars into the Japanese real estate market. Babcock & Brown; CB Richard Ellis; Cerberus Opportunity Funds; Citibank, N.A.; Colliers Halifax; Credit Suisse First Boston; GE Real Estate; GMAC Commercial Mortgage; Kennedy-Wilson; Lehman Brothers; Lonestar Funds; Moore Capital Partners; Morgan Stanley; Paribas; Secured Capital; Solomon Smith Barney; Soros Partners; and many others have been buying up prime commercial properties, some of which are 50 percent or more below their replacement cost.

These foreign investors are also investing in nonperforming loan pools secured by real estate, hard assets (direct property ownership), nonperforming pools of residential mortgages, unsecured corporate debts, and distressed companies undergoing bankruptcy proceedings. Such investments are very profitable because foreign investors can buy them from distressed sellers and face little competition from local buyers. Foreign investors also find that they can create value in commercial and residential properties by managing them more successfully.

Most Japanese banks are still gripped by the fear of repeating the debacle of the late 1980s, and are trying to avoid exposure to any activity that could lead to a capital loss. Japanese bankers also have a cultural reluctance to chase delinquent debtors. Major Japanese insurance companies and other traditional investors have been nursing their devastated property portfolios, and are in no mood to add new assets even if they could get funding. It is estimated that there is ¥700 trillion ($6.46 trillion) of commercial property in Japan, of which about 0.05 percent has been securitized to date. Of course, because of the extremely low interest rates on deposits and the poor performance of corporate bonds, Japanese investors are hungry for higher yields. Indeed, the Japanese real estate market is in desperate need of the liquidity that securitization can provide. In addition, foreign investors have found that Japanese banks have not been servicing mortgage assets effectively. They still have limited experience and professional expertise in dealing with secondary mortgage markets or real estate investment trusts. However, Japanese banks are now trying to learn new methods of real estate financing from foreign financial institutions, and are drastically altering the traditional ways of conducting their financing business.

Nonrecourse Financing

In recent years, a number of overseas financial institutions with operations in Japan—including Deutsche Bank, JP Morgan, Lehman Brothers, Morgan Stanley, and Shinsei Bank—introduced nonrecourse financing to both foreign and Japanese investors who were interested in securing this type of loan for real estate investments (see feature box on page 104).

Unlike traditional Japanese mortgage loans, nonrecourse financing is based primarily on the profitability of a real property rather than on the value of the property itself. It does not require additional collateral, a personal guarantee from the borrower, or cosigners. Instead, it requires proof of sufficient cash flow to determine market value. In other words, loan repayment is guaranteed by potential income from leases and by the proceeds from the future sale of the property. The collateral for this type of loan consists of the mortgage, an assignment of fire insurance, an assignment of lease rents, and a cash management agreement. The term for a typical nonrecourse loan is from five to seven years, but may be for only two years. Loan-to-value ratios are between 60 and 80 percent, depending on the lender's assessment of the subject property. Interest rates are currently 2.5 to 3.5 percent, although the specific rate is determined by the terms and conditions of each loan. Providers of nonrecourse financing usually require the following documents for review and evaluation of loan applications:

- A general description of the property;
- A location map;
- The certificate of title and official location map;
- Information on current tenants and lease terms: (1) the name of each tenant and a description of the area occupied by that tenant; (2) the lease period of each tenant; (3) the rent, common-area expenses, other charges, and amount of deposit;
- A detailed breakdown of annual income and expenses;
- The amounts of real estate tax, urban planning tax, and other taxes;
- Records of additions, major repairs, and equipment purchases;
- Vacancy rates;
- An appraisal report;
- A building inspection report, earthquake resistance report, and environmental assessment report;
- Both vertical and horizontal structural designs of the property.

Nonrecourse Financing from ORIX Corporation

Along with other Japanese financial institutions, ORIX Corporation has begun to provide nonrecourse financing to selected foreign and Japanese investors. Examples of some of the terms and conditions for nonrecourse loans from ORIX Corporation are shown in the accompanying table. These terms are for reference only.

Term Sheet for ORIX Nonrecourse Loans

Loan period	Five to seven years from the draw-down date.
Loan-to-value ratio	Between 60 and 80 percent of the lower of (1) the purchase price or (2) the value derived from an appraisal acceptable to the lender.
Prepayment	Not permitted for the initial period (known as the lockout period).
Interest rate	Three-month London Interbank Offered Rate + 150–300 basis points (1.5–3 percent) per annum (the actual rate will vary depending on a variety of factors)
Interest hedging	At closing, borrower is obligated to purchase, from a cap provider acceptable to the lender, an interest-rate cap for the life of the loan with a strike price that achieves a payment cap equal to 6.5 percent of the loan amount.
Front-end fee	1.0 percent of loan amount.
Processing fee	0.1 percent of loan amount, upon commitment by the lender.
Upfront reserves	Established at closing for any repairs, maintenance, or leasing commissions for substantial vacant space that are needed, in the reasonable judgment of the lender.
Security	• First mortgage or pledge on the trust beneficiary interest; • Pledge of the various bank accounts; • Assignment of tenant leases; • Pledge of the borrower's equity interest; • Assignment of insurance policies; • Pledge of the interest hedging agreement; • Minimum debt service coverage ratio covenant; • Financial covenants customary to transactions of this sort.
Expenses	Lender's legal fees and expenses, closing costs, stamp duty, mortgage registration tax, consumption tax, funding structure, third-party reports, and due diligence costs.
Recourse	No recourse to an entity controlling the borrower except in the event of fraud, misrepresentation, intentional damage, waste, misappropriation of funds, or unauthorized transfer of title to the mortgaged properties.
Monthly reserve	Reserves must be maintained in a separate bank account for property tax, sales tax, insurance, property maintenance, and capital expenditures. Other reserves may be established, based on the judgment of the lender.
Security deposit	Must be reserved in a separate account at closing.
Physical assessment report	A physical assessment report—including analysis of physical conditions, environmental risks, and seismic risks—must be undertaken prior to closing by a qualified and independent engineering firm acceptable to the lender.
Language of documentation	Japanese.
Jurisdiction	Tokyo District Court.
Governing law	Law of Japan.

Note: This list of terms and conditions is for illustrative purposes only and in no way represents a commitment or obligation by ORIX or any of its affiliates to provide this or any other financing.

The process of application and approval for a nonrecourse loan includes the following steps: submission of all required documents to the financial institution; thorough analysis of the application; issuance of major financing conditions; agreement on conditions; initiation of due diligence on the property; production of a financing contract and other documents (upon satisfactory completion of due diligence); signing of the contract and related documents; and implementation of the financing contract.

The conditions of a typical nonrecourse loan are as follows:

- Subject properties: rental office buildings, rental condominiums and apartments, shopping centers, hotels, and other commercial properties.
- Loan amount: approximately 70 percent of the appraisal value assigned by the financial institution's appraisers.
- Interest rate: variable (monthly London Interbank Offered Rate plus 3 percent).
- Loan period: three to five years.
- Prepayment: allowable, with prepayment penalty.
- Collateral: first mortgage, assignment of rental income, assignment of insurance proceeds, cash management agreement, etc.
- Loan origination fee: approximately 1 percent (depending on conditions).
- Borrower's expenses: due diligence fees, attorneys' fees, mortgage registration fee, and stamp tax. The due diligence fees include the appraisal fee, building inspection fee, earthquake-resistance testing fee, and environmental assessment fee.

Once due diligence has begun, all charges are paid by the borrower, to protect the financial institution in case financing is not completed for reasons that are not the fault of the financial institution. An estimate of due diligence charges can be obtained from the financial institution.

FIGURE 7-1

Comparison of a Traditional and Nontraditional Real Estate Loan

Elements of the Loan	Traditional	Nontraditional
Determination of value	Emphasizes land value	Emphasizes income
Major considerations in determining creditworthiness	Borrower's creditworthiness	Cash flow and assessed value
Cosigners	Required	Not necessary in principle
Collateral	Mortgage, assignment of fire insurance and life insurance proceeds, and cosigners	Mortgage, rental income, assignment of insurance proceeds
Default	Full recourse	No recourse

FIGURE 7-2

Benefits of a Nonrecourse Loan: A Hypothetical Case

	Self-Financing (in Millions of ¥, Unless Otherwise Indicated)	Nonrecourse Loan (in Millions of ¥, Unless Otherwise Indicated)
(A) Acquisition cost	1,000	1,000
(B) Portion of acquisition cost derived from nonrecourse loan	0	700
(C) Portion of acquisition cost derived from own capital	1,000	300
(D) Total investment: (B) + (C)	1,000	1,000
(E) Net cash flow	80	80
(F) Total interest	0	28
(G) Cash minus interest: (E) - (F)	80	52
(H) Return on investment: (G)/(C)	8%	17%

Cash Management System

To manage borrowers' funds, most financial institutions use a cash management system (known as a waterfall system) that distributes rental income according to predetermined priorities; the order is as follows: principal and interest account, deposit reimbursement reserve account, tax and insurance premium reserve account, management fee reserve account, repair and maintenance reserve account, tenant brokerage fee reserve account, and borrower's account. A servicer company affiliated with the financial institution often oversees the distribution of rental income, and may also provide other services such as loan management, asset resolution, foreclosure, and reporting to management and investors.

To ensure that the chance of investment bankruptcy is remote, a special-purpose company is often established in the Cayman Islands or some other tax haven. (A special-purpose company provides bankruptcy protection because it is treated as a separate entity from its originator for accounting and regulatory purposes.)

Securitization of Real Property

In June 1998, the Japanese diet passed the Special-Purpose Company (SPC) Law, which went into effect in September of that year. The law is important because it allowed, for the first time in Japan, the securitization of real property.

FIGURE 7-3

Servicer Companies

Servicer Company	Affiliated Company
A-co Servicer Company, Ltd.	—
ACS Credit Management Corporation	AEON Credit Service Company, Ltd.
Adhoc Servicer, Inc.	—
AIC Saiken Kaishu Kabushiki Kaisha	—
AIP Saiken Kanri Kaisyu	—
Amic Services Company	Hitachi Capital Corporation
Amresco Japan, Inc.	Amresco, Inc.
Aozora Loan Service Company, Ltd.	Aozora Bank, Ltd.
Asahi Servicer Company, Ltd.	Asahi Bank, Ltd.
ASO Saiken Kabushiki Kaisha	—
Astry Loan Services Corporation	Aiful Corporation
Asuka Servicer Company, Ltd.	—
Atrium Servicing Company, Ltd.	Atrium, a subsidiary of Credit Saison Company, Ltd.
BM Asset Management Company	—
BOTL Servicer Company, Ltd.	BOT Lease Company, Ltd.
Capital Servicing Company, Ltd.	—
CCC Collection Services, Inc.	Japanese law firm
Central Servicer Company, Ltd.	—
Century Servicing Company, Ltd.	Banking companies
CF Saiken Kaishu	Central Finance
Chiba Servicer Company, Ltd.	Chiba Bank, Ltd.
CM Servicing Corporation	—
Cooperative Servicing Company, Ltd.	Norinchukin Bank
Credit Guarantee Servicer, Inc.	—
DC Services Company, Ltd.	DC Card Company, Ltd.
Frontier Servicer Company, Ltd.	APLUS Company, Ltd.
Fukuoka Saiken Kaishu Kabushiki Kaisha	Fukuoka Bank, Ltd.
Global Asset Management Company, Ltd.	Cargill, Inc., and First City Servicing Corporation
GMAC Commercial Mortgage Japan K.K.	GMC GMACCM
Hudson Japan Saiken Kaisyu K.K.	Hudson Advisor
Ibayu Saiken Kaishu Kabushiki Kaisha	—
IR Loan Servicing, Inc.	ACOM Company, Ltd. (60%); Risa Partners Inc. (40%)
IT Servicer Company, Ltd.	—
Jaccs Loan Collection Service Company, Ltd.	Jaccs Company, Ltd. (Japan Consumer Credit Service)
Japan Collection Service	Orient Corporation
Japan Finance Saiken Kaisyu	—
Japan Leasing Service Corporation	General Electric Capital Corporation
Japan Payment Network Company, Ltd	Credit Saison Company, Ltd.
Justice Saiken Kaishu	—
Kyushu Servicer Corporation	—
LNR Partners	—
Lombard Servicing, Inc.	A foreign investor
MCS Saiken Kanri K.K.	Daiei OMC, Inc.
Minato Debt Collection K.K.	Goldman Sachs
Minerva Collection Agency, Inc.	ITX Corporation
Miyako Saiken Kaishu Kabushiki Kaisha	—

Continued

FIGURE 7-3

Servicer Companies (continued)

Moore SVP Management Corporation	—
MTK Servicer Company, Ltd.	—
Nichiboshin Servicer, Ltd.	—
Nihon Revival Saiken Kaishu Kabushiki Kaisha	Phoenix Capital Company, Ltd.
Nissin Servicer Company, Ltd.	Nissin Company, Ltd.
Nittaku Trust Saiken Kaishu Kabushiki Kaisha	Nittaku Group
Nittele Credit Collection Company, Ltd.	Nihon Tele Search
NS Servicer Company, Ltd.	Nippon Shinpan Company, Ltd.
Okayama Saiken Kabushiki Kaisha	—
Okinawa Collection Service Company, Ltd.	Oaks Company, Ltd.
ORIX Asset Management and Loan Services Corporation	ORIX Corporation
Pacific Servicer Company, Ltd.	Kennedy-Wilson Japan K.K.
PAL Servicer Company, Ltd.	Promise Company, Ltd.
Premier SKK	A foreign investor
Resolution and Collection Corporation	—
Ricres Company, Ltd.	Ricoh Leasing Company, Ltd.
S.S.J. Saiken Kaishu Kabushiki Kaisha	—
Sakura Servicing Company, Ltd.	SMBC Bank, Ltd.
San-in Saiken Kaishu Kabushiki Kaisha	San-in Godo Bank
Sanwa Servicer Company, Ltd.	Sanwa Finance Inc.
Sanyo Shinpan Service Corporation	Sanyo Shinpan Finance Company, Ltd.
SCJ Servicer Company, Ltd.	Secured Capital Japan Company, Ltd.
Shimanami Servicing Company, Ltd.	Hiroshima Bank
SMBC Loan Servicer Company, Ltd.	SMBC Bank, Ltd.
Sogo Saiken Kaishu Company, Ltd.	Dai-Ichi Kangyo Bank, Ltd.
Tokyo Diamond Servicer Company, Ltd.	Bank of Tokyo-Mitsubishi, Ltd.
Tokyo Servicer, Inc.	Tokyo Real Estate Investment Consulting, Inc.
Toranomon Saiken Kaishu	Nittaku Group
Ukoh Saiken Kaisyu	—
Workout Servicer Company, Ltd.	—
Yamabiko Services Company, Ltd.	Hachijuni Bank, Ltd.
Yamada Servicer Synthetic Office	—
Yamato Servicing K.K.	Cerberus Japan K.K.
Yashio Servicing Company, Ltd.	Ashikaga Bank, Ltd.

Notes: Information is current as of October 2003. (—) indicates that the information is unavailable. The names of servicer companies that do not have English names have been transliterated.

The law's major aim was to increase the liquidity and marketability of nonperforming real estate loans and depressed real properties; to that end, it permits the securitization of specified assets, such as real estate, and provides the securitization of rights to beneficiary interest from a real estate trust. Figure 7-3 lists examples of real property securitization in the Japanese market. Since 1998, many companies, both domestic and foreign, have securitized their real estate assets in Japan.

The SPC Law provides tax advantages on the profits from real estate transactions. SPCs are exempt from corporate tax if they pay out over 90 percent of their earnings as dividends. The law also allows a reduction in the real property acquisition tax (from 3 percent on both land and buildings to 0.5 percent for land and 1.5 percent for buildings). This reduction is in effect until March 31, 2005. There is also a reduction in the registration and license tax, and total exemption from the special landholding tax.

SPCs are allowed to issue three kinds of asset-backed securities: preferred-equity stocks, specified bonds, and commercial paper. To establish an SPC, the minimum capital requirement is ¥100,000 ($924), reduced from ¥10 million ($92,340) in 2000. Under the SPC law, an SPC can be treated as being off the balance sheet of the originator, and is also bankruptcy remote with respect to the originator.

SPCs enhanced the establishment of Japanese real estate investment trusts (J-REITs). The end of the bubble economy forced many real estate companies to choose between either bankruptcy and dissolution or going public to gain access to capital markets.

Japanese Real Estate Investment Trusts

The Japanese government passed revisions to the Investment Trust Law in November 2000, and the Tokyo Stock Exchange drew up listing criteria for J-REITs in March 2001. Subsequently, the Investment Trusts Association came up with rules for J-REITs (see feature boxes on page 113 and 114). The listing of the first J-REIT, in the summer of 2001, was an extremely significant development in that it created a new secondary market for securitized products based on real estate.

J-REITs have the following five basic characteristics (detailed legal and tax ramifications have been omitted):

- Real estate investments are allowed under the framework for investment trusts (investment companies that until recently were limited to mainly marketable securities).
- Borrowing, debt insurance, equity issuance, and the cancellation of shares are permitted.
- Dividends can be deducted from earnings, as long as more than 90 percent of income is distributed to investors as dividends. (This arrangement effectively exempts J-REITs from the corporate tax.)

FIGURE 7-4

The Process of Securitization

Release Date	Asset	Originator or Loan Creditor	Property/Asset Type
February 2002	Apartment development project	DYNACITY Corporation (developer)	Apartments
March 2002	Tobu Ikebukuro, Tobu Funabashi, and others	Tobu Department Store Company, Ltd.	Department store and other properties
March 2002	TWIN 21 (in Osaka Business Park) and other properties	Matsushita Investment & Development Company, Ltd.	Office building
March 2002	Four nonrecourse loans on 17 office properties	Bank of Tokyo-Mitsubishi, Ltd.	Nonrecourse loans
March 2002	Four office buildings	Yasuda Real Estate Company, Ltd.	Office buildings
March 2002	Three office buildings	Yasuda Real Estate Company, Ltd.	Office buildings
March 2002	KDDI Data Center	KDDI Corporation	Data center
April 2002	Seven rental apartment buildings	Secured Capital Japan Company, Ltd.	Apartments
April 2002	Don Quijote Roppongi	Don Quijote Company, Ltd.	Retail store
April 2002	Headquarters of the former Nippon Credit Bank and four other buildings	Multiple creditors	Office building and other properties
April 2002	Atami Beach Line	Mitsui Kanko Development Company, Ltd.	Toll road
April 2002	Hankyu Grand Building and other properties	Hankyu Corporation	Mixed-use building
June 2002	Nine nonrecourse loans on 14 properties	J.P. Morgan Securities Asia Pte. Limited	Nonrecourse loans
August 2002	Nine nonrecourse loans on 12 properties	Morgan Stanley	Nonrecourse loans
August 2002	29 properties (mainly office buildings)	J.P. Morgan Securities Asia Pte. Limited	Office buildings
August 2002	Central business hotel and other properties	Amms International	Business hotel, rental housing
August 2002	40 properties	ORIX Corporation	Not available
December 2002	Eight leisure facility properties	Round One Corporation	Leisure facilities
December 2002	Nonperforming loans	Shinsei Multi Asset Recovery Transaction Company, Ltd.	Nonperforming loans
February 2003	A loan against 25 apartment properties	Morgan Stanley	Loan
March 2003	Seven apartment buildings, two retail buildings, one parking lot	Orient Corporation and others	Various

a. Figures in this column may not equal the total amount of funds secured through the securitization of assets, and are presented only for reference, to give an idea of the scale of the transaction.
b. Information on the value of the beneficial interests in trust is not readily available.

Location	Value (in Billions of ¥/Millions of $) of Financial Instruments Issued against Securitized Assets[a]
Minato Ward, Tokyo	0.9/8.07 in corporate bonds[b]
Funabashi City and other locations	8.39/77.4 in corporate bonds[b]
Osaka and Tokyo	39.9/363.9 in corporate bonds[b]
N.A.[d]	25.8/235.4 in corporate bonds[b]
Tokyo	5.1/47 in corporate bonds[c]
Tokyo and Funabashi City	7.5/69.2[c] (4.7/43.3 in the form of a nonrecourse loan)
Meguro Ward, Tokyo	14.2/131 (nonrecourse loan)[b]
Tokyo	16.9/155.9 in corporate bonds[b]
Minato Ward, Tokyo	4.2/38.8[b]
Tokyo, Fukuoka City, Hiroshima City, Kanazawa City	40/369[c]
Atami City	12/110.7 in corporate bonds[b]
Umeda Ward, Osaka, and other locations	52/47.9 in corporate bonds[b]
N.A.	34.8/321[c]
N.A.	15.7/144.8 in corporate bonds[b]
Tokyo	17.8/164.2 in corporate bonds[b]
Tokyo	3.4/31.4 in corporate bonds[b]
Tokyo	19.9/183.5 in corporate bonds[b]
Not available	9.6/88.5 in corporate bonds[b]
N.A.	13.4/123.6 in corporate bonds[b]
N.A.	15.05/138.8 in corporate bonds[b]
Not available	8/73.8 in corporate bonds[b]

c. Valuation of beneficial interests in trust at time of transfer.
d. Not applicable.

■ J-REITs are marketable securities that, under the Securities Exchange Law, can be listed on the Tokyo Stock Exchange.
■ Investment companies are legally required to contract out real estate management to third-party fund managers.

All these characteristics are important, but the most significant is the use of a Tokyo Stock Exchange listing to create (1) securitized real estate instruments intended for secondary distribution and (2) a market for such instruments. In Japan, real estate has yet to gain full acceptance as an investment vehicle, but in the near future it will be viewed as an asset class on a par with bonds or equities.

Debt Collection and Management Companies

In 1993, a special law was enacted that allowed the establishment of debt collection and management companies *(saiken kaishu kanri kaisha)*. The purpose of the law was to expedite settlement of a large number of bad loans that had been accumulated by banks and other financial institutions since the collapse of the bubble economy. The law was also intended to increase the liquidity of real properties by allowing the prompt settlement of bad real estate loans.

Until passage of this law, only Japanese lawyers were allowed to

FIGURE 7-5

Corporate-Style Investment Trust

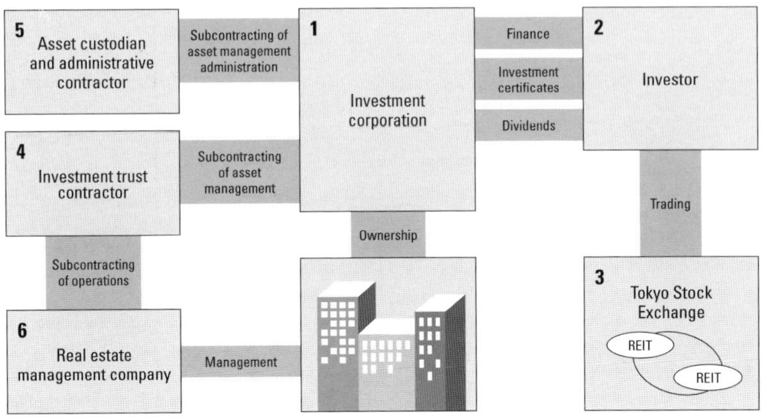

Source: *Tokyo Stock Exchange.*

1. Investment corporation: Investment corporations are special entities specifically established to own and manage real estate, using investors' money. Like any other company, an investment corporation has an executive board and holds shareholder (investor) meetings. Having a board and holding shareholder meetings are necessary for the corporation to own and manage real estate, and are the only permissible activities for such corporations.
2. Investor: Investors entrust funds to the investment corporation in return for investment certificates, which are equivalent to shares. Investors holding investment certificates at the end of the financial period are entitled to dividend payments, just as if they held shares.
3. Tokyo Stock Exchange: The Tokyo Stock Exchange (TSE) lists and provides a marketplace for Japanese real estate investment trusts (J-REITs). J-REIT investment certificates can be freely traded on the TSE during standard trading hours, and are subject to the same trading regulations as stocks.
4. Investment trust contractor: Investment trust contractors are responsible for managing the J-REIT assets on behalf of the investment corporation; in other words, they fulfill an important role as fund managers. Investment trust contractors are generally involved from the establishment of the investment corporation, and from then on manage the corporation's real estate assets, buying and selling as necessary to get the best returns.
5. Asset custodian and administrative contractor: Trust banks maintain custody of assets (in reality, custody of rights certificates), on behalf of the investment corporation. Assets are held in segregated accounts. Other administrative duties, such as the registration of investment-certificate holders and the issuance of new certificates, are carried out by investment trusts and securities companies on behalf of the investment corporation.
6. Real estate management company: Real estate management companies handle all aspects of the direct management of the real estate assets so as to maximize long-term returns; their responsibilities include the handling of rental contracts and invoices and the physical management of the properties.

engage in the collection of bad loans and the settling of bad debts—a legal limitation that had created an extraordinary backlog of settlement cases. The Ministry of Justice, under the Special Implementation of the Law Regarding Debt Collection and Management (Saiken Kanri Kaishu Ni Kansuru Tokubetsu Shochiho), is now able to issue licenses to private companies that can meet the conditions specified for this type of business activity.

Listing Criteria for Real Estate Investment Trusts on the Tokyo Stock Exchange

Because investments in real estate investment trusts (REITs) are being undertaken as an alternative to direct investment in real estate, the main focus of the Tokyo Stock Exchange REIT listing criteria is on the nature and proportion of real estate assets held within the fund.

Assets under Management

- Real estate must make up at least 75 percent of total assets under management.
- Assets must be real estate–related, cash, or highly liquid cash equivalents.
- At least 50 percent of total assets must be income producing, and not likely to be sold within a year.

Fund

- Real estate must make up at least 75 percent of total assets under management.
- Total assets must be at least ¥5 billion ($46.2 million).
- Net assets per unit must be at least ¥50,000 ($460).

Distribution

- At least 4,000 units must be listed.
- At least 1,000 units, shareholders, or investors are required.
- Major units or shareholders may hold no more than 75 percent of listed units.

Source: *Adapted from information provided by the Tokyo Stock Exchange.*

To qualify for a license, a debt collection and management company must have a capitalization of more than ¥500 million ($4.6 million), and one of the directors must be an attorney; in addition, the company must have in place specific measures to exclude the involvement of gangsters *(yakuza)*. The major business activities of such companies are the collection and/or management of bad debts on behalf of banks, postal savings associations, credit card companies, farmers' cooperatives, fishery associations, insurance companies, and other organizations.

Debt collection and management companies must abide by the strict code of ethics stipulated by the Ministry of Justice. The companies are prohibited from (1) using verbal or physical intimidation tactics that might threaten the life of the debtor, (2) employing a gangster or asking for his assistance, (3) using false information or illegal means to obtain settlement, (4) resorting to false announcements or exaggerated advertisements, and (5) having an attorney pursue a judgment. In other words, the debt collection and management company

Disclosure Requirements for REITs on the Tokyo Stock Exchange

Real estate investment trusts (REITs) are subject to disclosure requirements similar to those imposed on stocks, including those that concern the investment corporation (issuer) and underlying assets.

Investment Corporation

Investment corporations are required to disclose decisions concerning the issue and sale of additional units, and the undertaking of a unit split. Other matters to be disclosed include the receipt of orders to improve operations, and information about fund management contractors.

Assets under Management

Any adjustment over a certain level of assets under management must be disclosed. In particular, the following must be disclosed:

- The transfer of 10 percent or more of net assets;
- A profit or loss that results from a transfer of assets and is equivalent to 30 percent or more of that period's gross profits;
- A loss that results from damage from a natural disaster and that is equivalent to 3 percent or more of net assets;
- A profit/loss or dividends that differ from the original forecast by 30 percent or more or 20 percent or more, respectively.

Financial Results

Just as for stocks, investment corporations are required to issue *tanshin*—reports giving summaries of their financial results once they are finalized. These reports include (1) the value of assets under management and (2) forecasted dividends.

Investment corporations are legally required to disclose details of the real estate properties they hold (including the use and value of each property), as well as of the revenues from tenant properties (including the number of tenants, for example). Investors also receive annual management reports about the REITs they own, allowing them to monitor how well they are managed.

Source: *Tokyo Stock Exchange.*

is a legitimate loan collection company authorized by the Minister of Justice and under the minister's close supervision.

Debt collection and management companies can be a good source for finding suitable investment properties with nonperforming loans, although some of them are subsidiaries of major Japanese and foreign finance companies, and therefore work mainly for their parent companies.

Court Auction System

To solve the problem of disposing of the large number of nonperforming loans, the Japanese Ministry of Justice has improved the court auction system (*fudosan keibai tetsuzuki*). However, the Japanese foreclosure and auction system remains different from that of the United States. In Japan, a creditor or lender cannot force the sale of a property outside of the court system to recover the funds lent to the debtor, as is done in the United States. Instead, the creditor has two means of generating repayment: one is to entice the debtor to sell the property voluntarily, and the other is to petition the court for a judicial foreclosure.

In the case of a judicial foreclosure, the court announces a forthcoming auction *(keibai)* and allows potential buyers to examine documents relating to the property, a court-requested appraiser's report, and details of any rent contracts, which the buyer must take over. Unlike the approach used in the United States, the court also sets a minimum foreclosure price for the property, based on the appraisal. Buyers are informed of this price before the auction, and it becomes the basis for submitting bids. Bids are not open and competitive; instead, during the bidding period, each potential buyer submits a sealed bid to the court that includes a 20 percent deposit of the minimum bid price or an agreement from a financial institution guaranteeing payment. The court announces the highest bidder after the bidding period has closed, and ownership of the property is transferred to the highest bidder once full payment has been received.

After all the court costs and other expenses have been paid, the net proceeds of the sale will be divided among the creditors according to the agreement. Although it is a cumbersome system, it may be one of the most effective means for foreign investors to acquire depressed real properties in Japan at a substantial discount.

Note

1. A project financing arrangement is a nonrecourse or limited-recourse financial structure in which the debt and equity used to finance the project are paid back from the cash flow generated by the project itself. Project financing is used to support long-term infrastructure, industrial projects, or public services.

Chapter 8

Taxes Applicable to Foreign Investors

Japan's taxation system differs, to some extent, from that of the United States and other countries. Japan imposes unique taxes on the acquisition, sale, holding, registration, and conveyance of real estate, as well as other special taxes. There are also different kinds of corporate taxes levied on foreign companies and individuals doing business in Japan. Foreign investors must become familiar with Japanese taxes in order to successfully carry on business activities in Japan.

Foreground: The 333-meter (1,092-foot) Tokyo Tower, which was built in 1958. Background: The Mori Tower Building stands out from the recently developed ¥273 billion ($2.5 billion) Roppongi Hills project.

Taxes on Real Estate

Municipal, prefectural, and national governments impose seven major taxes on real estate transactions and ownership: the real property acquisition tax *(fudosan shutoku zei)*, the consumption tax *(shohi zei)*, the special landholding tax *(tokubetsu tochihoyu zei)*, the registration and license tax *(toroku menkyo zei)*, the stamp tax *(inshi zei)*, the fixed-asset tax *(koteishisan zei)*, and the urban planning tax *(toshikeikaku zei)*.

Real Property Acquisition Tax

The real property acquisition tax is assessed by municipal and prefectural governments and applies to buyers of land and buildings. Land includes residential land, farmland, salt beds, mineral mines, wetlands, forests, pastures, and raw land. Buildings include homes and apartments, office buildings, stores, factories, and warehouses. In the case of land with a building on it, tax is calculated separately for the land and for the building, then totaled. "Real estate acquisition" refers to the transfer of real property ownership rights through purchase, exchange, gift, inheritance, donation, contribution in kind, new construction, additions, reclamation, and other forms of transfer.

The current rate of taxation is basically 4 percent of the assessed value of a real property, as registered in the fixed-asset tax registry. However, temporary legislation has reduced the tax rate to 3 percent until March 31, 2006. Furthermore, until December 31, 2005, half of land valuation has been excluded from the taxable base. There is also a lump-sum allowance for new houses. For example, a new residence with a floor area of between 50 and 240 square meters (between 540 and 2,585 square feet) can receive a tax exemption of ¥12 million ($110,650). Such housing incentives were designed to encourage homeownership among middle-income Japanese households, and are not meant for investors and speculators dealing with large real properties.

Consumption Tax

The consumption tax is similar to the general excise tax or sales tax found in almost all states in the United States. The 5 percent tax rate is a combination of national and local taxes (4 percent and 1 percent, respectively) and is charged on the construction contract price, brokerage commissions, and rental income from office or store leases. Thus, for example, the tax assessment for a fee-simple office building would be based on the value of the building portion only; the land is exempt. Another exemption is given for income from residential leases. The consumption tax can be a substantial sum in the case of multimillion-dollar real estate purchases.

Special Landholding Tax

The special landholding tax, which applies to those who either hold or purchase a parcel of land of more than a specified size, is 1.4 percent for landowners and 3 percent for buyers. In specified metropolitan districts, including Tokyo's 23 wards, the tax applies to properties that are larger than 2,000 square meters (21,530 square feet); in City Planning Areas, the tax applies to properties that are larger than 5,000 square meters (53,820 square feet); and in other cities, towns, and villages, it applies to properties that are larger than 10,000 square meters (107,640 square feet.)

Tax reforms passed in 2003 have temporarily suspended the special landholding tax. The original intent of the tax, however, was to discourage landowners from holding onto good residential land parcels for the purpose of speculation and land banking. For example, the owners of open-air parking lots or small farms situated in densely populated city centers are penalized by this tax. However, exemptions are given for land transactions that include buildings or promote the construction of a building within a reasonable period of time. It is important to note that in the case of a new land purchase, purchasers can deduct the amount of real property acquisition tax from the amount of special landholding tax owed. In addition, landowners can deduct the amount of fixed-asset tax from the amount of special landholding tax owed.

Registration and License Tax

The registration and license tax is a national tax paid when real property is registered for retention or transfer of ownership, or when a mortgage is registered. For retention of ownership, the tax rate is 0.2 percent (until March 31, 2006, and 0.4 percent thereafter) of the value of the real property; for transfer of ownership, it is 1 percent (until March 31, 2006, and 2 percent thereafter); and for registration of mortgages, it is 0.4 percent of the amount of debt. The assessment is based on the assessed value of real property as recorded in the official registry.

Stamp Tax

The stamp tax is similar to the conveyance tax used in the United States, and is paid when real estate purchases, sales contracts, construction contracts, rental agreements, and leases are registered. The stamp tax is a national tax charged

FIGURE 8-1 **Stamp Tax Duties per Sales Contract**

Contract Amount (¥/$)	Stamp Tax per Document (¥/$)
Under 100,000/920	200/1.80
100,000–500,000/920–4,610	400/3.70
500,000–1,000,000/4,610–9,220	1,000/9.20
1,000,000–5,000,000/9,220–46,115	2,000/18.40
5,000,000–10,000,000/46,115–92,225	10,000/92.30
10,000,000–50,000,000/92,225–461,130	15,000/138.40
50,000,000–100,000,000/461,130–922,260	45,000/415.20
100,000,000–500,000,000/922,260–4,610,940	80,000/738.20
500,000,000–1,000,000,000/4,610,940–9,221,870	180,000/1,660.80
1,000,000,000–50,000,000,000/9,221,870–461,086,280	360,000/3,321.70
50,000,000,000/461,086,280 and over	540,000/4,983.60

per document and is based on the nature and amount of the transaction. Stamp tax assessments for sales contracts are as shown in figure 8-1.

Fixed-Asset Tax

The fixed-asset tax is imposed by local governments on registered owners of land or buildings. The standard tax rate is 1.4 percent, but each municipality is allowed to set its own tax rate, not exceeding 2.1 percent. The assessed value of real property is usually 70 percent of the posted price *(koji kakaku)*, but is reassessed every three years.

FIGURE 8-2

Tax on the Purchase of an Existing Office Building: An Illustrative Example (¥)

1. Transaction price	600,000,000
2. Values recorded in the fixed-asset registry	
Land	220,000,000
Building	200,000,000
Total	420,000,000
3. Calculation of tax amount	
Real property acquisition tax	
Land: 3%[a] of 220,000,000 x .5[b]	3,300,000
Building: 3% of 200,000,000	6,000,000
Subtotal	9,300,000
Registration and license tax	
Land: 1%[c] of 220,000,000	2,200,000
Building: 1%[d] of 200,000,000	2,000,000
Subtotal	4,200,000
Stamp tax[e]	180,000
Total	**13,680,000**

a. Until March 31, 2006; 4% thereafter.
b. The reduction by one-half is applicable to land purchased before December 31, 2005.
c. Until March 31, 2006; 2% thereafter.
d. Until March 31, 2006; 2% thereafter.
e. Applies to contract values between ¥500,000,000 and ¥1,000,000,000.

In recent years, special measures have been taken to reduce the taxable portion of residential land transfers that meet specific requirements. For example, small parcels of residential land (less than 200 square meters—2,155 square feet) are assessed at one-sixth of the registered land price. For new houses built by March 31, 2006, the assessment for the first 120 square meters

(1,290 square feet) of total floor area is reduced by one-half for the first three years of ownership.

Urban Planning Tax

The urban planning tax is a yearly local tax imposed by municipalities on owners of land or buildings located within areas subject to urban planning. Each municipality is allowed to set its own tax rate, but it may not exceed 0.3 percent of the assessed value of the property. There are special measures to reduce this tax burden for smaller properties. For example, for small parcels of residential land, the taxable base is reduced by one-third; for very small parcels of residential land, it is reduced by two-thirds.

Corporate Taxes

The taxable income of a corporation depends on whether it is a domestic or a foreign corporation. If a foreign corporation establishes a subsidiary or joint venture whose main office is in Japan, the subsidiary or joint venture is regarded as a domestic corporation; if a foreign corporation establishes a branch office or representative office in Japan, that office is regarded as a foreign corporation. While a domestic corporation is required to pay corporate tax on all income from its worldwide operations, it is permitted to apply for tax credits for income taxes paid outside of Japan, allowing it to avoid double taxation. On the other hand, a foreign corporation is required to pay corporate tax only on income generated in Japan according to the following guidelines:

■ A foreign corporation with a branch office in Japan is required to pay corporate tax on all domestic-source income (that is, income generated from any business in Japan, income generated from assets in Japan, and any other income whose source is in Japan) and to file a tax return based on the tax treaty between Japan and its home country. (Japan currently has tax treaties with 55 countries.) Exceptions to this rule are as follows: a representative office of a foreign company engaged in advertising, gathering information, market surveying, basic research, and other supplementary activities in Japan is not required to pay corporate tax. Furthermore, remittance of funds from the Japanese branch to its home office and transactions between them are generally not subject to corporate taxation.

■ A foreign corporation (1) that is directly engaged in construction or supervision of construction in Japan for more than one year, or for the period specified

FIGURE 8-3

Withholding Tax Rates and Rates under Tax Treaties (%)

Recipient	Dividends: Portfolio	Dividends: Substantial Holdings[a]	Interest[b]
Japanese corporations	20	20	20
Resident individuals	20 or 35[e]	20	20[f]
Nonresident individuals and nontreaty foreign corporations[g]	20	20	15 or 20
Withholding tax rates under tax treaties			
Australia	15	15	10
Austria	20	10	10
Belgium	15	10	10
Brazil	12.5	12.5	12.5
Canada	15	10	10
Czech Republic	15	10	10
Denmark	15	10	10
Egypt	15	15	15
Finland	15	10	10
France	15	0 or 5	10
Germany	15	10	10
Hungary	10	10	10
India	15	15	10 or 15
Indonesia	15	10	10
Ireland	15	10	10
Israel	15	5	10
Italy	15	10	10
Malaysia	15	10	10
Mexico	15	0 or 5	10 or 15
Netherlands	15	5	10
New Zealand	15	15	15 or 20
Norway	15	5	10
Pakistan	20	15	0, 15, or 20
Peoples' Republic of China	10	10	10
Philippines	20	10	10 or 15
Poland	10	10	10
Republic of Korea	12	12	12
Russia	15	15	10
Singapore	15	5	10
South Africa	15	5	10
Spain	15	10	10
Sweden	15	10	10
Switzerland	15	10	10
Thailand	20	15 or 20	10, 15, or 20
Turkey	15	10	10 or 15
United Kingdom	15	10	10
United States	15	10	10

Source: National Tax Agency, Japan, and Japanese External Trade Organization.

Notes: Data are current as of June 2003. Because of space limitations, the table does not include all countries with which Japan has tax treaties.

a. The tax treaty rates apply only to corporate shareholders. The applicable treaty should be checked for conditions required to claim the reduced rate.

b. Tax rates on interest differ in certain tax treaties, depending on the source or recipient of the interest. The applicable treaty should be checked for the appropriate rates.

c. The applicable treaty should be reviewed; certain tax treaties exclude from taxable income film royalties, cultural royalties, gains from the transfer of copyright, etc.

d. Not applicable.

e. The 35 percent rate applies if, under certain conditions, the taxpayer elects not to aggregate this income with other sources of income.

f. Beginning April 1, 1988, interest on bank deposits and/or certain designated financial instruments became subject to a 15 percent national withholding tax and a 5 percent local inhabitants' withholding tax (20 percent combined). Because the taxation of such interest is taken care of entirely through withholding, resident individuals are not required to aggregate such interest income with other sources of income. Interest on loans made

Royalties[c]
N.A.[d]
N.A.
20
10
10
10
12.5, 15, or 20
10
0 or 10
10
15
10
10
10
0 or 10
20
10
10
10
10
10 or 20
10
10
20
10
0
10
10, 15, or 20
0 or 10
12
0 or 10
10
10
10
10
10
15
10
10
10

by resident individuals is not subject to withholding tax; instead, it is aggregated with other sources of income and then taxed.

g. Dividends, interest, and/or royalties earned by nonresident individuals or foreign corporations are subject to a 20 percent withholding tax under Japanese domestic law. An exceptional rate of 15 percent is applied to interest on bank deposits or designated financial instruments accruing on or after April 1, 1988. Interest on loans, however, is taxed at a 20 percent rate, even after March 31, 1988.

in the tax treaty, or (2) that is doing business through an agent who is authorized to conclude contracts, is required to pay corporate tax on income derived from these business activities.

■ A foreign corporation that receives income from the sale of real estate is required to deduct corporate tax from this income.

■ Income earned by a foreign corporation in Japan from interest, dividends, or royalties is subject to withholding tax. If Japan has a tax treaty with the home country of a foreign corporation, the treaty may reduce the rate of tax withholding from a high of 20 percent to 15, 10, 5, or even 0 percent.

Japanese corporations making certain payments are required to withhold income tax at varying rates that depend on whether the recipient is a Japanese corporation, a resident individual of Japan, a nonresident of Japan, or a foreign corporation. The rates are also affected by tax treaties. Figure 8-3 provides detailed information on withholding rates and tax treaties.

The calculation of corporate income for tax purposes must be made according to the generally accepted accounting practices in Japan. The fiscal year is the period specified in the articles of incorporation, although a common fiscal year in Japan is from April 1 to March 31. Typically, corporate income is classified into six different categories: dividend income, profit from revaluation of assets, revenue from ordinary sales, income from installment sales, profit from long-term construction contracts, and capital gains from the sale of fixed assets. Expense items are categorized as cost of sales; cost of completed construction;

selling expenses; administrative expenses; other expenses and losses; taxes paid; salaries, wages, and bonuses; entertainment expenses; donations; and losses from bad debts. Depreciation of buildings is calculated on a straight-line method according to the following schedule: reinforced concrete buildings for office use, 50 years; for residential use, 47 years; for hotel use, 39 years; and for factory use, 38 years. (If the main structure of the building is steel or wood, other figures are stipulated for each type of use.)

One important aspect of taxation in Japan is that the Japanese government does not look kindly on countries that provide tax havens and has implemented special measures to counter such practices. These measures apply in the following circumstances: if a company is incorporated outside of Japan and one or more Japanese residents or companies hold over 50 percent of that company's issued shares, it is classified as a "foreign-related company." If such a company is based in a tax-haven country that has a corporate tax rate of 25 percent or less, any resident of Japan or any Japanese domestic corporation that owns 5 percent or more of that company will be taxed on the income of the foreign-related company; that is, the income will be deemed to have been generated in Japan. However, these measures do not apply to a foreign subsidiary that owns fixed assets in and conducts business from a tax haven, and that meets other stipulated requirements.

Taxes on corporate income consist of the corporate tax *(hojin zei)* imposed by the national government; the corporate residence tax *(hojin jumin zei)* imposed by the prefectural and municipal governments; and the corporate

FIGURE 8-4

Tax Burden on Corporations: Illustrative Example, 2002

	Income before tax (in millions of ¥/thousands of $)		
	Up to 4/36,920	**4–8/36,920–73,800**	**Over 8/73,800**
Corporate tax (%)	22.00	22.00	30.00
Corporate residence tax			
Prefectural (%)	1.10	1.10	1.10
Municipal (%)	2.70	2.70	3.68
Corporate enterprise tax (%)	5	7.30	9.60
Total tax rate (%)	30.80	33.10	44.38
Effective tax rate[a] (%)	29.33	30.85	40.86

a. The effective rate is the tax rate after an allowance has been made for the enterprise tax, which is treated as a loss.

enterprise tax *(hojin jigyo zei)* imposed by the prefectural government. The corporate tax and the corporate residence tax are not deductible when calculating corporate income, but the corporate enterprise tax is treated as a loss.

Corporate tax rates for corporations capitalized at not more than ¥100,000,000 ($921,940) are as follows:

■ 22 percent for the portion of annual income up to ¥8,000,000 ($73,755);

■ 30 percent for taxable income over ¥8,000,000 ($73,755)

■ For corporations capitalized at more than ¥100,000,000 ($921,940), 30 percent of all taxable income.

Gains from the sale of land or leasehold are subject to an additional 6 percent tax on top of the ordinary corporate tax. If the land or leasehold interest is sold within five years after acquisition, the additional tax is 12 percent of the gains. However, this special taxation has been suspended until December 31, 2008.

Corporate residence tax is levied on both Japanese and foreign corporations that have established their businesses in Japan. The tax rate is 17.3 to 20.7 percent of total corporate tax payments, but corporations must also pay a per capita corporate residence tax of between ¥70,000 ($645) and ¥3,800,000 ($35,000), depending on the amount of capitalization and the number of employees.

The corporate enterprise tax is levied on both Japanese and foreign corporations that have a permanent office or business establishment in the prefecture to pursue business. The tax rates are:

■ Between 5 and 5.25 percent for taxable corporate income under ¥4 million ($36,900);

■ Between 7.3 and 7.665 percent for income between ¥4 million ($36,900) and ¥8 million ($73,800);

■ Between 9.6 and 10.08 percent for income over ¥8 million ($73,800).

A uniform tax rate of between 9.6 and 10.08 percent is levied on corporations that have a capitalization of at least ¥10 million ($92,200) and are engaging in business activities in three or more prefectures. If the sum of paid-in-capital and capital surplus exceeds ¥100 million ($921,900), an additional enterprise tax will be assessed, based on the amount of capitalization and adjusted income.

Chapter 9

The Surge in Foreign Investment in Commercial Properties

Since the late 1990s, overseas investors have been investing aggressively in Japanese real estate. Although falling land prices have certainly been one of the main reasons for the large influx of overseas investment, there are a number of other factors as well, including the following:

■ The continuing disposal, by financial institutions, of a larger and larger volume of nonperforming loans backed by real estate;

■ The disposal of nonessential real estate assets by Japanese corporations;

■ Opportunities to acquire and turn around heavily indebted or liquidated companies;

■ New government support measures to encourage more investment from overseas;

- Deregulation, simplification, and modernization of building-related laws;
- A steep fall in construction costs (caused by stiff competition among general contractors);
- The introduction of creative project financing and nonrecourse lending;
- Changes in accounting rules to provide greater financial transparency;
- Reductions in real estate–related taxation;
- The introduction of asset securitization legislation and the establishment of the real estate investment trust (REIT) market;
- The increased use of the income approach for the appraisal of assets;
- Relative stability in Japanese income and spending patterns.

In recent years, some of the world's largest retailers—including Carrefour SA, of France, and Costco Wholesale Corporation and Wal-Mart Stores Inc., of the United States—have entered the Japanese market and attracted a great deal of media attention. The popularity of American-style outlet malls and theme shopping centers has also attracted major U.S. REITs, such as Chelsea Property Group, Inc., to Japan. The rapid expansion of the U.S. coffee-shop operator Starbucks, and others like it, has also been remarkable, bringing fundamental changes to Japan's coffee-shop industry.

Despite difficult economic times, the love affair that many Japanese shoppers have with luxury European goods has continued unabated. Cashing in on this bonanza, luxury retailers have bought up properties in prime city-center locations, where they have built ever-larger and more sophisticated stores. Meanwhile, a substantial number of luxury hotels, funded by overseas investors, are under construction in Tokyo. Many are being built as part of larger urban development projects; of these, several are in Tokyo's five central wards and were developed during 2002 and 2003.

According to Mori Building, a private development firm, just over 2 million square meters (21,527,830 square feet) of new office space was added in Japan in 2003—a figure that is roughly equivalent to the total for 2001 and 2002 combined. Many more projects are slated to be constructed in the next decade, several of which are being financed by overseas funds such as Alderney Investments Pte. Ltd., of Singapore. In the existing-property market, large U.S. investment banks such Goldman Sachs and Morgan Stanley, as well as investment funds such as Lone Star Group and AIG Group, are some of the largest investors.

The Changing Tokyo Skyline

With a large number of urban redevelopment projects currently underway, Tokyo is in the process of undergoing a major face-lift. A number of factors have made these projects possible. First, several large tracts of land in central Tokyo have become available for commercial development projects. Second, a decline in the prices of both land and construction has made investing in such projects more profitable for domestic and foreign investors alike. The last time Tokyo witnessed such an expansion in office space was in 1994.

According to an office market report released by Ikoma/CB Richard Ellis in January 2004, the supply of new office buildings in Tokyo's 23 central wards was 1.14 million square meters (12.27 million square feet) in 2003; the only time a higher figure was recorded was during Japan's economic bubble. The same report projects 446,000 square meters (4.8 million square feet) of new office space for 2004. Despite worries about the impact of the large amount of new office space on office vacancy rates, the vacancy rate for 2003 (6.9 percent) was only 0.8 percent higher (relative to the volume of supply) than it had been the previous year.

The Shinagawa project was developed on a 16-hectare (40-acre) site that was previously used as a rail yard. The project includes two condominium towers and three new office buildings that house the headquarters and subsidiaries of several Mitsubishi companies. The project is located beside Shinagawa Station, a train station through which 730,000 people pass each day.

The gradual recovery of the Japanese economy appears to be supporting the unexpectedly strong demand for office space. The largest office developments are being undertaken in the Shinagawa, Shiodome, and Roppongi districts.

The Shinagawa project is being developed on a 16-hectare (40-acre) site that was previously used as a rail yard. Mitsubishi Corporation, Mitsubishi Motors, and Mitsubishi Heavy Industries have each built a new, 31- or 32-story office tower at the site. The area houses over 450,000 square meters (4,843,760 square feet) of office space. The project also includes two condominiums with 830 units and a total floor area of almost 115,000 square meters (1,237,850 square feet).

Shiodome, located on the waterfront near Shinagawa, is the site of another major redevelopment project that includes ten office buildings with a total floor area of 1,176,000 square meters (12,658,365 square feet). In 2002, the project began to open in stages, starting with the Shiodome Dentsu Building, the headquarters of Dentsu, Japan's largest advertising agency. The other buildings, which will open as they are completed, include three large-scale condominiums, a theater, and the headquarters of several other major Japanese corporations, among them Kyodo News Service and Matsushita Electric. Alderney Investments Pte. Ltd., a Singaporean investment firm, is putting up the financing for the construction of Shiodome City Center—which, with a total floor area of 187,745 square meters (2,020,870 square feet), is the largest office building in the project.

Mori Building recently finished the Roppongi Hills project, the third major project in Tokyo's Roppongi district. The project, which opened in April 2003, features a total of 11 buildings, including a 54-story office building, four high-rise condominiums, a museum, a theater, and a hotel. The project's 840 residential units account for almost 150,000 square meters (1,614,585 square feet) of the project's total 724,500 square meters (7,798,455 square feet). The project, situated on an 11-hectare (27-acre) site, is not only an office zone but also a place where people can live, work, and play both day and night. Of the ¥280 billion ($2.58 billion) spent on the project, almost ¥180 billion ($1.67 billion) was provided in nonrecourse loans through an arrangement designed by Mizuho Securities; the financing scheme involved 14 financial institutions, including the government-affiliated Development Bank of Japan.

Other large-scale redevelopment projects are also underway in the western part of Roppongi and in the area surrounding Kachidoki, in the Chuo ward.

FIGURE 9-1

Acquisitions of Japanese Assets by Non-Japanese Firms

	Foreign Purchaser	Japanese Seller	Asset Type
February 2002	Chanel K.K.	The Daiei, Inc.	Office building
January 2003	Lone Star Group	Chisan Company, Ltd.	Operator of 16 golf courses and 25 hotels
January 2003	Goldman Sachs	The Daiei, Inc.	Four hotels
February 2003	ProLogis Japan Fund	Kawasho Soko, Ltd.	Distribution center
March 2003	Kennedy-Wilson Japan K.K.	N.A.[a]	Office buildings
March 2003	Gucci Group NV	Kinki Nippon Railway	Office building
June 2003	Tiffany & Co.	Iwasaki Group	Office building
September 2003	IKEA Japan	Mitsui Fudosan Company	Former indoor ski slope
December 2003	Morgan Stanley	The Daiei, Inc.	Shinkobe Oriental Hotel
December 2003	ABM Property Corporation	N.A.	Two distribution centers
January 2004	Lone Star Group	Holiday Tower Company	Two hotels
February 2004	Goldman Sachs Group	Japan Promotions, Inc.	Operator of 28 golf courses
February 2004	ABM Property Corporation	Unifood, UF Soko (a subsidiary of Unifood)	Two distribution warehouse
March 2004	Morgan Stanley	Daikyo Incorporated	Office building
March 2004	ProLogis Japan Fund	Urban Development Corporation	Land
March 2004	Colony Capital LLC	The Daiei, Inc.	Sports dome and hotels

a. Not available

The Kachidoki project includes four office buildings and nine condominiums with 1,800 residential units.

Investment in office property is likely to increase even further as the number of REITs listed on the Tokyo Stock Exchange (TSE) increases. UBS AG, the Swiss-based financial conglomerate, and Mitsubishi Corporation listed Japan's third REIT on the TSE on March 12, 2002. One REIT affiliated with Mitsui Fudosan and another affiliated with Mitsubishi Estate (these are Japan's two largest real estate companies) were listed on the stock market in 2001.

Overseas investment banks and funds such as Goldman Sachs, Morgan Stanley, Merrill Lynch, Bankers Trust, Schroeders, AIG Group, and Lone Star Group have become major investors in Japanese real estate in recent years. In

Asset Location
Ginza, Tokyo
All over Japan
Chiba, Fukuoka, Kobe, and Osaka prefectures
Uruyasu City, Chiba Prefecture
Hiroshima City and Sendai City
Ginza, Tokyo
Ginza, Tokyo
Funabashi City, Funabashi Prefecture
Kobe City
Saitama Prefecture
Aichi and Kyoto prefectures
All over Japan
Chiba and Funabashi prefectures
Chiyoda Ward, Tokyo
Yokohama City
Fukuoka City

November 2001, Goldman Sachs sold back the Yamato Seimei Building, located next to the Imperial Hotel, in central Tokyo, to its original owner, Yamato Mutual Life Insurance Company, for an estimated ¥59.1 billion ($545 million). In 1997, when foreign buyers were considerably fewer than they are today, Goldman Sachs drew a great deal of media attention when it purchased the building. (Figure 9-1 lists some acquisitions of Japanese properties by overseas firms.)

Luxury Retailers Acquire Prime Retail Locations

In recent years, as they expanded their businesses in the Japanese market, overseas luxury retailers have started to invest aggressively in Japanese real estate. While overall retail sales have fallen in recent years, expenditures on luxury brands have increased. Industry analysts point out that consumers are focusing expenditures on either very low-priced everyday items or on high-priced luxury items, while products in the middle have been losing out. In 2002, the 44 stores of Louis Vuitton Japan KK reached ¥135.7 billion ($1.25 billion) in sales, a gain of 15.1 percent over sales for the previous year. Louis Vuitton Japan's taxable income rose to ¥32.4 billion ($299 million) from ¥25.6 billion ($237 million) over the same period.

Buoyed by strong sales, European fashion houses such as Louis Vuitton, Prada, Hermès, and Chanel have revised their sales strategies, remodeling existing outlets or building large flagship stores in prominent locations, such as Tokyo's Ginza and Omotesando districts. In many cases, larger flagship stores allow luxury-brand makers to provide a greater variety of products and better customer service than the outlets traditionally located within department stores. Flagship stores also give luxury-brand firms greater control over their image than is the case for in-store outlets, where the image of the department store itself is important. In many instances, overseas retailers have decided to purchase rather than to lease the property on which they have their new stores.

At the same time that they are opening new flagship stores, many luxury retailers are also expanding existing stores and opening new stores in major cities outside of Tokyo. Gucci Group NV announced in April 2003 that it had acquired a premium site in Tokyo's Ginza district from a local Japanese railway company, Kinki Nippon Railway. Gucci intends to demolish the existing building and replace it with a new, 4,800-square-meter (51,670-square-foot) building that will include a 1,000-square-meter (10,765-square-foot) flagship store and 3,800 square meters (40,905 square feet) of office space for Gucci Group Japan's headquarters. The site has a total area of 438 square meters (4,715 square feet). While the financial terms of acquisition were not disclosed, the *Nikkei Shimbun* reported in April 2003 that the publicly disclosed land price of a neighboring building was ¥15.7 million per square meter ($13,454 per square foot), the second-highest price ever paid for a commercial land plot in Japan. In 2001, Gucci increased the size of its outlet within the Matsuzakaya department store, in Ginza, by 200 percent, to 500 square meters (5,380 square feet). In 2003 Gucci opened new outlets in department stores located outside of Tokyo; among the cities with new outlets are Sapporo, Niigata City, and Wakayama City.

Tiffany & Co., of the United States, announced in June 2003 that its Japanese subsidiary had purchased the land and building of its flagship store in Tokyo's Ginza district for ¥16.5 billion ($152 million). The nine-story building has a total floor area of approximately 5,667 square meters (61,000 square feet), of which the flagship store occupies approximately 1,115 square meters (12,000 square feet).

In 2002, in a deal reported to be worth ¥17.4 billion ($160 million), Chanel K.K., the Japanese subsidiary of the French fashion conglomerate, agreed to purchase the Ginza Building from the Daiei, Inc., a large Japanese supermarket operator. Located in Tokyo's Ginza district, the building has eight stories aboveground and one underneath, and some 5,500 square meters (59,200 square feet) of total floor space. In 1998, Hermès Japan, the Japanese arm of the French luxury-goods maker, purchased a property in Ginza—where, in June 2001, it opened its largest store in Japan to date. Designed by Renzo Piano and built by Takenaka Corporation, the new 14-story Hermès store has a total floor area of 6,040 square meters (65,015 square feet).

In 2002 and 2003, the pace of store openings by high-end brands in Ginza was strong, and is likely to continue. Overseas luxury brands that opened new flagship stores in Ginza in 2002 included Agnona, Coach, Lancel, and Lladro. In 2003, a. testoni, Barneys New York, Cartier, Lazare Kaplan, Prada, Salvatore Ferragamo, St. John's, and Zara all opened new Ginza stores. In February 2004, Lanvin opened a new flagship store on Ginza's main street. Chanel, Christian Dior, and Gucci have announced plans to open new stores between 2004 and 2005.

Several luxury retailers have recently opened new stores in Tokyo's Omotesando district, helping to further boost the area's image. In a little over a year, LVMH Moët Hennessy Louis Vuitton, the world's largest luxury-goods company, opened two large stores on Omotesando Dori Avenue, Tokyo's answer to Paris's Champs-Elysées. Louis Vuitton opened its largest store in the world on Omotesando Dori on September 1, 2002. The flagship store, housed in a new building with a total floor area of 3,330 square meters (35,845 square feet), has a retail floor area of 1,240 square meters (13,350 square feet). The store recorded sales of ¥125 million ($1.2 million) on its first day of business, a record for a Louis Vuitton store. The store is built on land acquired by the LVMH Moët Hennessy Louis Vuitton Group. On September 20, 2003, the LVMH Group opened another new, large-scale flagship store at the top of

An award-winning retail complex in the trendy Harajuku-Omotesando neighborhood. The building, which includes the largest Gap store outside the United States and a number of international restaurants, was developed by Takenaka Corporation.

Omotesando Dori. The new store, named "ONE Omotesando" because of its prominent location, houses four of the group's non–Louis Vuitton brands: Celine, Donna Karan New York, Fendi, and Loewe. The flagship store has a total floor area of approximately 1,600 square meters (17,220 square feet), with two floors aboveground and one below.

On the same street, Christian Dior also opened a new store at the end of 2003. Other brands, such as Gucci and Chanel, already have stores on Omotesando Dori. In June 2003, Italian luxury retailer Prada opened a new flagship store just off Omotesando Dori, at a site that the company had acquired from a Japanese bank in 1999. The store, shaped like a crystal and covered on all sides by a glass facade, has a total area of 2,800 square meters (30,140 square feet).

In 2003, LVMH Moët Hennessy Louis Vuitton acquired an additional site, formerly occupied by a Japanese department store, in Osaka's Shinsaibashi district. Also in 2003, Louis Vuitton opened a new outlet within the Kintetsu Department Store, in Wakayama City.

In September 2003, Saks Incorporated, of the United States, announced that beginning in 2004, it plans to open Saks Fifth Avenue stores in Japan. The first Japanese branch of this luxury department store chain is scheduled to open in Tokyo in the fall of 2005, with a total floor space of approximately 5,000 square meters (53,820 square feet). Saks plans to enter the Japanese market through an agreement with a consortium of Japanese fashion specialty stores, a developer, and retail consulting companies, which will own and operate the stores under a licensing agreement with Saks Fifth Avenue.

Arrival of Large-Scale Overseas Retailers

In recent years, large-scale supermarket operators have entered the Japanese market one after another. In this group, Tesco Plc., of the United Kingdom, is the latest arrival. Tesco announced on July 11, 2003, that it had successfully acquired over two-thirds of the outstanding shares in C Two-Network Co., a mid-sized Japanese supermarket. C Two-Network operates 78 supermarkets, mainly around Tokyo, and posted sales of ¥48.9 billion ($452.5 million) in fiscal 2002, with a pretax profit of ¥3.5 billion ($32.5 million). Wal-Mart, the world's largest retailer, entered the Japanese market in March 2002 by acquiring a 6.1 percent stake in Japan's fourth-largest supermarket chain, the Seiyu,

Ltd. By September 2003, Wal-Mart had increased its stake in Seiyu to 37.8 percent and held the option to increase its stake to 66.7 percent by 2007. While Wal-Mart had yet to open any of its own stores by the end of 2003, by August 2003 Seiyu had fully implemented Wal-Mart sales methods and information systems.

Carrefour SA, of France, the world's second-largest retailer, opened its first Japanese store in Makuhari, Chiba Prefecture, in December 2000. Less than a week later, Costco Wholesale Corporation, a U.S. membership store, opened its second store in Japan nearby. (Costco had opened its first Japanese store in the Fukuoka Prefecture, in southern Japan, in April 1999.)

While falling land prices have been a key factor in attracting overseas retailers, they have certainly not been the only one. Greater flexibility on the part of local governments in dealing with overseas retailers and the gradual consolidation of Japan's multilayered distribution system have also acted as incentives for overseas players. In 1998, for example, to promote the entry of retailers to its advanced commercial district, in Makuhari, the Chiba prefectural government abandoned its traditional policy of only *selling* land, and instead implemented a new leasing system.

The changes that have occurred in Japan's distribution system over the past decade stem primarily from two factors: advances in information technology and the onslaught of price discounting that began in the early the 1990s. According to a government report—*Japan's High-Price Myth in the Process of Collapse*—issued in 2000 by the Economic Planning Agency, "Japan's multilayered distribution network is slowly being transformed as wholesalers consolidate and direct transactions between producers and retailers grow." The report noted that in the food industry, between 1988 and 1997, the average number of wholesalers in the chain between producers and retailers fell from 1.81 to 1.68. During the same years, in the medicine and cosmetics sector, the number also fell below 1.7.

Despite an overall reduction in the number of wholesalers at different levels, the transformation of the distribution system is still in the early stages. For example, overseas retailers like Carrefour, which have sought to procure goods directly from suppliers, have found many to be unresponsive. Nevertheless, while many companies have resisted pressures from both foreign and domestic retailers to sell to them directly, others have not. For example, in October 1999,

Hep Five, an innovative, award-winning, ten-floor shopping mall in Osaka, Japan. The mall's hallmark is a giant Ferris wheel, based on the seventh floor, that stands out against the Osaka skyline.

Procter & Gamble broke with a 27-year tradition and began to deliver its products directly to major supermarket chains.

By 2003, Carrefour had opened seven stores in Japan, including one in Akashi City, in western Japan. Unlike Carrefour's previous stores, which were built from the ground up, to the company's specifications, this store is located in a building that was previously occupied by a Japanese supermarket chain. Carrefour is leasing the land and building from the landowner.

By the end of 2003, Costco had opened four stores in Japan and had plans to open a number of new stores within two years. In the spring of 2002, Costco and Carrefour joined forces to open a new shopping center in Amagasaki, in Hyogo Prefecture, in western Japan. On a 49,500-square-meter (532,815-square-foot) site, Costco built a one-story store with a total floor area of approximately 13,000 square meters (139,930 square feet). Costco rents the remainder of the site to Carrefour, which built a two-story hypermarket with 20,000 square meters (215,280 square feet) of floor space.

In April 2001, Metro AG, a membership wholesaler from Germany, set up a joint venture company with Marubeni Corporation, a Japanese trading company, to enter the Japanese market. In December 2002, Metro opened its first store in Chiba, east of Tokyo; in February 2003, it opened a second store in Kawaguchi, Saitama Prefecture, with a 5,000-square-meter (53,820-square-foot) sales floor.

Specialty large-scale retailers have also begun to enter the Japanese market. IKEA, the Swedish-based furniture retailer, announced in 2002 that it was re-entering the Japanese market. IKEA originally entered in 1974 but withdrew in 1983 because of disappointing sales. IKEA plans initially to open four to six stores around Tokyo, then to open a similar number of stores in western Japan, near Osaka. The first IKEA in Japan will open in September 2005, in Funabashi, east of Tokyo, on land that the company plans to acquire, and will have a sales floor area of approximately 30,000 square meters (322,920 square feet).

Payless Shoes, of the United States, which directly operates approximately 5,000 large-scale discount shoe stores in 13 countries in the Americas, plans to open its first store in Japan in 2004. In October 2003, the U.S. retailer established a joint venture company with one of Japan's largest trading houses, Nichimen Corporation.

As overseas players make their first moves into the Japanese market, mergers among Japanese retailers are also taking place. The AEON Group acquired the fifth-largest supermarket group, Mycal, after its bankruptcy. This takeover has made AEON Japan's largest supermarket chain in terms of sales. AEON has proven that innovative retailers can be successful in Japan despite Japan's continued economic problems. Beginning in fiscal 2004, AEON plans to open as many as 100 new food-centered supermarkets.

Ito-Yokado, operator of Seven-Eleven stores, also increased sales in its domestic supermarkets during 2002. Ito-Yokado is more conservative in its expansion plans than AEON, concentrating instead on increasing revenue and profitability at existing supermarkets. Even Ito-Yokado's total sales, however, are dwarfed by Wal-Mart's: in the fiscal year ending in January 2004, Wal-Mart recorded worldwide sales of ¥26.4 trillion ($256.3 billion)—almost nine times those of Ito-Yokado.

Strong Sales for Factory Outlet–Style Malls

Despite overall sluggishness in the retail market, Chelsea Property Group, Inc., a U.S. mall operator, has enjoyed considerable success in Japan. In 1999, Chelsea established a joint venture company, Chelsea Japan Company, with

Mitsubishi Estate, a Japanese real estate company, and Nissho Iwai, a Japanese trading company. Chelsea Japan opened its first outlet mall, Gotemba Premium Outlets, some 90 kilometers (56 miles) southwest of Tokyo, in Shizuoka Prefecture, in the summer of 1999. One of the major attractions of the Japanese market for Chelsea was that Japanese visitors already accounted for some 10 percent of the 60 million people who visited the company's 24 malls in the United States every year.

Gotemba Premium Outlets has over 80 stores, many of which are run directly by well-known companies such as Gap and Brooks Brothers, of the United States; Swiss leather-goods maker Bally; and Nina Ricci and Trussardi, of Italy. The mall attracted some 2 million visitors in its first 50 days, with sales totaling some ¥6.5 billion ($60 million). Total sales for the year reached some ¥30 billion ($27.7 million), while the number of visitors topped the 6 million mark. Chelsea further expanded the Gotemba mall in July 2003, making it the largest mall in Japan.

In November 2000, Chelsea Japan opened a second outlet mall, Rinku Premium Outlet, near Osaka. Phase II of the project was completed in March 2002. Chelsea added a third outlet mall, Sano Premium Outlet, in March 2003. Sano Premium, with a total area of 33,909 square meters (364,995 square feet), is located near the popular tourist areas of Nikko and Nasu Kogen, which attract an estimated 6.5 million visitors per year. Chelsea recently announced that it would open a fourth outlet mall in Tosu, Saga Prefecture, in southern Japan, in spring 2004. Plans for a fifth outlet mall, in Toki, Gifu Prefecture, have also been announced. Ultimately, Chelsea plans to operate between eight and ten outlet malls in Japan.

Overseas Hotel Owners Invest in Tokyo

There has been a recent noticeable increase in the number of foreign hotel chains entering the Japanese hotel market as investors or operators. Tokyo, in particular, has seen a rapid rise in the number of foreign-operated luxury-hotel chains. New hotels include the Sofitel Tokyo (opened by the French hotel-chain operator Accor Group, in September 2000); the Four Seasons Marunouchi (a 57-room hotel that opened in October 2002); and the Grand Hyatt (which opened in April 2003, as part of the Roppongi Hills development). Future entrants include the Mandarin Oriental (in Nihonbashi); the Peninsula Hotel (in the Hibiya Park Building); the Marriott Ritz-Carlton (in Roppongi); and the St. Regis (in the Shiodome area).

Hotel-industry experts believe that the top end of Tokyo's market still has room to grow, given the relative scarcity of luxury hotels in the city. Foreign hotel chains hope to attract a greater number of young Japanese women and foreign business executives who are familiar with their hotels overseas. The recent rush in hotel development can be attributed, in large part, to the fact that a number of redevelopment projects are currently being undertaken in central Tokyo, and project developers have been vigorously courting luxury-hotel operators. Foreign corporations are also aggressively purchasing existing Japanese hotel chains and resorts.

After the complex filed for bankruptcy in February 2001, Ripplewood Holdings LLC stepped in to acquire the Seagaia resort, in Miyazaki Prefecture, for a reported ¥16.2 billion ($149.5 million). The Seagaia resort is Japan's largest recreational complex, boasting 1,100 rooms, an indoor ocean dome, a convention hall, golf courses, and other facilities. Ripplewood appointed Starwood Hotels & Resorts as its lodging-facilities and guest-attractions operator. Starwood is using its Sheraton Resorts brand name for the hotels.

Another overseas company investing in Japan's hotel market is Soros Real Estate Partners, a real estate investment company run by George Soros. The company set up a Japanese subsidiary, Ishin Hotels Group, in 2001, and has already purchased two hotels, the Hilton Narita New Tokyo International Airport Hotel and the Kyoto Royal Hotel.

The Surge in Overseas Food-Service Businesses

The tremendous success of Starbucks since 1995, when it first set up operations in Japan, has had a dramatic influence on Japan's coffee-shop industry. With 467 outlets as of June 2003, Japan is Starbucks' second-largest market after North America. In fiscal 2003, sales in Japan rose 9 percent, to ¥59.2 billion ($546.5 million), while the company posted a parent-only net profit of ¥180 million ($1.6 million). Starbucks returned to profit in 2003, after suffering a loss in the previous year, by aggressively cutting material and store-operation costs and selecting new store locations more carefully. Starbucks opened its 500th store in November 2003, in Nagoya; new store openings will continue in 2004.

The success of Starbucks has enticed a host of other overseas coffee shops and restaurants to enter the Japanese market. Tully's Coffee Japan, with 130 stores as of September 2003, is Japan's second-largest specialty coffee-shop operator. Tully's has a licensing agreement with Tully's Coffee Corporation, of the United States, which supplies coffee beans to the company. The company expects sales in 2003 to reach close to ¥9 billion ($83 million) as it continues to rapidly add stores throughout Japan.

Other overseas coffee-store operators, such as Segafreddo Zanetti, of Italy, and Best Coffee, of the United States, are also slowly expanding their presence in Japan. Young women, in particular, have been attracted to these new-style coffee shops, which are more spacious and have a more relaxed ambience than traditional Japanese coffee shops.

Dean & DeLuca, a specialty-foods chain, has also entered the Japanese market, opening its second store in October 2003, in the Shibuya district, after an extremely successful launch of the first Dean & DeLuca store in the Marunouchi district.

Rainforest Café, a U.S. theme restaurant, opened its first store in the Ikispari shopping mall, near Tokyo's Disneyland, in July 2000. The interior of the store is decorated with computer-controlled replicas of wildlife animals, such as gorillas and elephants, and includes an aquarium and a waterfall. Many overseas restaurant operators are faced with the challenge of how best to adapt their product to appeal to Japanese tastes. RC Japan, the operator of Rainforest Café, for example, has changed the seasonings it uses in its Japanese menus, reduced portions by around 30 percent, and added a greater variety of fish to its menu.

T.G.I. Friday's Japan, a joint venture between Carlson Restaurants Worldwide, Inc., of the United States, and Watami Food Service Company, of Japan, has also added a number of local items such as teriyaki burgers and yakitori (skewered grilled chicken) to its menu. After some consideration, the company decided, however, to keep American sized-cocktail drinks, which have more than twice the volume of traditional Japanese cocktails. A large number of other overseas food-service companies, including Hard Rock Café, Lawry's, and Subway, are also expanding their businesses in Japan.

Conclusion

Japan's real estate industry is in an advanced stage of liberalization that resulted from the Japanese government's efforts to encourage direct overseas investments. Not long ago, Japanese laws restricted the acquisition and ownership of real properties in Japan by foreign interests. However, the recent financial crises and the subsequent restructuring of traditional Japanese banks have forced the government to open doors to foreign investors. Many foreign corporations have already invested billions of dollars in Japanese real properties. Indeed, because the Japanese economy has recently begun showing strong signs of recovery, this may be the best time ever to invest in Japanese real properties.

Many factors are attracting international investors to Japan. For example, Japan is the second-largest economy in the world, and is well known for high productivity and innovations. The real estate industry currently ranks as the third-largest economic activity, after automobile and electronics manufacturing. Furthermore, the Japanese government has become more enthusiastic about encouraging foreign direct investment and has enacted legislation to help facilitate such investment.

While the collapse of Japan's bubble economy brought about a number of positive changes in the country's real estate market, the need for overseas investors to be familiar with unique Japanese practices and customs has not diminished, as is outlined in chapter 1. One of the greatest difficulties that investors face in the Japanese real estate market is finding property to acquire. Efforts to create a transparent listing system for real properties in Japan are still in the early stages: word-of-mouth information and personal connections still remain very important. Real estate brokers and lawyers perform services similar to those undertaken by their Western counterparts, although they often become involved at a later stage of the process.

Chapter 2 illustrates the fact that negotiation remains very much an art in Japan, and includes an array of rituals and idiosyncrasies that need to be understood and appreciated by overseas investors. Investors also need to be aware that because of Japan's unique market characteristics, Japanese appraisal methods differ from those used in other parts of the world. Government indices provide guidelines for prices in real estate transactions but need to be used carefully in combination with private appraisals. As highlighted in chapter 3, the income approach, common in the United States, has come into wider use in Japan, particularly in conjunction with the cost approach and the market comparison approach.

As explained in chapter 4, building, zoning, and structural safety restrictions in Japan are also influenced by unique characteristics, such as the relative scarcity of land, the risk of earthquakes, and historical practices. Building codes and zoning ordinances can seem quite rigid; it is therefore important to know how to discuss these codes with the local authorities who apply them.

Chapter 5 explains the conditions found in a typical Japanese land, building, office, and residential lease, and highlights the unique features of such leases—such as the length of the lease term, the payment of key money and rental agents' fees, and the need for joint surety or guarantors.

In Japan, real properties are recorded in the registry book in the district where the property is located, as outlined in chapter 6. Recording of real property transfers, leasehold rights, and mortgages is not mandatory; however, except for leases, almost all such transactions are recorded, in order to protect the rights of the parties involved. There are no escrow or title insurance companies in Japan, and it is therefore important to conduct a thorough title search on all properties. All records of real estate transactions are open to the public.

In recent years, new legislation and the increased participation of overseas financial institutions in Japan's real estate market have led to the expansion of real estate financing methods. As highlighted in chapter 7, legislation that opened the way to the securitization of assets and the creation of a real estate investment trust market has also brought considerable fluidity and flexibility to the Japanese real estate market. Increasingly, overseas firms in Japan obtain debt financing not only from overseas financial institutions with offices in Japan but also from domestic Japanese firms. And in recent years, nonrecourse financing, which is based on the profitability of real property rather than on land value, has enjoyed growing popularity in Japan.

Chapter 8 describes the Japanese taxes that affect foreign investors. As in any country, prudent investors must consider the tax consequences of their decisions in order to minimize risk and maximize opportunities.

Chapter 9 describes the many redevelopment projects taking place in Japan and lists some of the overseas retailers and investors that have entered the Japanese market. Foreign companies from a variety of industries—including retailers, hotel owners and operators, and food-service companies—are currently enjoying strong financial success in Japan and are anticipating promising futures.

The Japanese economy is showing tangible signs of recovery, and the Japanese government's legislative reforms are creating numerous opportunities for foreign investors interested in entering the Japanese market. There is clearly significant potential not only today, but also for many years to come.